President
Theodore Roosevelt's
Conservation Legacy

W. Todd Benson

Copyright © 2003 by W. Todd Benson

ISBN 0-7414-1611-5

Published by:

PUBLISHING.COM

519 West Lancaster Avenue
Haverford, PA 19041-1413
Info@buybooksontheweb.com
www.buybooksontheweb.com
Toll-free (877) BUY BOOK
Local Phone (610) 520-2500
Fax (610) 519-0261

Printed in the United States of America

Printed on Recycled Paper

Published August 2003

President Roosevelt unites in himself powers and qualities that rarely go together. Thus, he has both physical and moral courage in a degree rare in history. He can stand calm and unflinching in the path of a charging grizzly, and he can confront with equal coolness and determination the predaceous corporations and money powers of the country.

He unites the qualities of the man of action with those of the scholar and writer,- another very rare combination. He unites the instincts and accomplishments of the best breeding and culture with the broadest democratic sympathies and affiliations. He is as happy with a frontiersman like Seth Bullock as with a fellow Harvard man, and Seth Bullock is happy, too.

He unites great austerity with great good-nature. He unites great sensibility with great force and power. He loves solitude, and he loves to be in the thick of the fight. His love of nature is only equaled by his love of the ways and marts of men.

John Burroughs
Camping With President Roosevelt,
The Atlantic Monthly (May 1906)

TABLE OF CONTENTS

PREFACE

Years ago, while I was directing the activities of The Robert R. Merhige Jr., Center for Environmental Studies at the University of Richmond, an irascible law professor (and friend of mine) would ask, "Todd, how can you be a Republican and an environmentalist?" Professor Wade Berryhill's taunts caused me to read my first biography on Teddy Roosevelt. I enjoyed the story and the man but I wanted to learn more about President Roosevelt's environmental activities, the reason I read the biography in the first place. This led to the next biography and then the next.

My respect for the 26th president of the United States grew while my basic mission remained largely un-accomplished. Finally, at my wife's suggestion, I began to write the book I that I had set out to read.

Teddy Roosevelt was a phenomenally charismatic and energetic president, a good and kind man with extraordinary talent and drive. As one biographer wrote, the "great paradox of Roosevelt's character was the contrast between its fundamental simplicity and its apparent spectacular quality."[1]

Roosevelt spoke in superlatives: the best he had ever seen, or the biggest, or the most remarkable, or simply bully. While breakfasting at Memphis' Maxwell House, the President was asked if he would like more coffee. "Delighted," he is said to have responded. "This coffee is good to the last drop." One friend supposedly chided the President: "Theodore, if there is one thing more than every other for which I admire you, it is your original discovery of the Ten Commandments."

Roosevelt's unbounded exuberance for life included his dealings with executives and dignitaries. He developed a game during childhood: go as far as you could in a straight line crossing ravines, scaling precipices, and fording lakes and rivers, but always go onward and forward.

Roosevelt continued this form of exercise and amusement while President. Gifford Pinchot, Roosevelt's forester, friend, and environmental advisor, claimed that when a new member of the administration's inner circle came to Washington, the President would test his mettle with a hike. "More than one soft-muscled chair warming Army or Navy officer failed to meet that test."[2] One day, Roosevelt invited the newly arrived French ambassador, M. Jusserand, to hike with him. Mind you, this was at a time when people "called" and were properly attired when so doing – "a black cut away coat, striped trousers, and the rest of the regular calling uniform."[3] The experience of the French ambassador presumably is chronicled in a dispatch reported on by author and Roosevelt contemporary William Roscoe Thayer:

> "Yesterday,… President Roosevelt invited me to take a promenade with him this afternoon at three. I arrived at the White House punctually, in the afternoon dress and silk hat, as if we were to stroll in the Tuileries Garden or in the Champs Elysees. To my surprise, the President soon joined me in a tramping suit, with knickerbockers and thick boots, and soft felt hat, much worn. Two or three other gentlemen came, and we started off at what seemed to me a breakneck pace, which soon brought us out of the city. On reaching the country, the President went pell-mell over the fields, following neither road nor path, always on, on, straight ahead! I was much winded, but I would not give in, nor ask him to slow up, because I had the honor of La

belle France in my heart. At last we came to the bank of a stream, rather wide and too deep to be forded. I sighed relief, because I thought now we had reached our goal and would rest a moment and catch our breath, before turning homeward. But judge of my horror when I saw the President unbutton his clothes and heard him say, 'We had better strip, so as not to wet our things in the Creek.' Then I, too, for the honor of France, removed my apparel, everything except my lavender kid gloves. The President cast an inquiring look at these as if they, too, must come off, but I quickly forestalled any remark by saying 'With your permission Mr. President, I will keep these on, otherwise it would be embarrassing if we should meet ladies.' And so we jumped into the water and swam across."[4]

The President delighted in the good humor of the ambassador. He and the ambassador bonded and, with Roosevelt, France had the ear of the White House.

Roosevelt instituted and maintained a policy of wise use of the nation's resources. Although the phrase "wise use" has a negative connotation to many environmentalists today, it was a necessary and proper doctrine for the time. Indeed, "wise use," as defined by Roosevelt and Pinchot, is today recognized as "sustainability," which is in the forefront of environmental objectives worldwide. Then, as now, the nation needed wood and other resources; then, as now, the trick was to timely replenish renewable resources and to protect against wasting nonrenewable ones. Even the great John Muir recognized and apparently approved of the wise use concept: "In their natural condition or under wise management, keeping out destructive sheep, preventing fires, selecting the trees that should be cut for lumber, and preserving the young ones and the shrubs and sod of herbaceous vegetation, these forests would be a never failing fountain of wealth and beauty."[5]

Roosevelt came to the White House (the name he placed on the "Executive Mansion") with a deep and abiding love of nature, including its animals, its places, its plants, and its moods. It is impossible to read Roosevelt's work and not recognize this aspect of the man. His writing sings with the beauty he found in nature:

"One of our sweetest, loudest songsters is the meadow-lark...the plains air seems to give it a voice, and it will perch on the top of a bush or tree and sing for hours in rich, bubbling tones."

"Nowhere, not even at sea, does a man feel more lonely than when riding over the far-reaching, seemingly never-ending plains; and after a man has lived a little while on or near them, their very vastness and loneliness and their melancholy monotony have a strong fascination for him."

"Nothing could be more lonely and nothing more beautiful than the view at nightfall across the prairies to these huge hill masses, when the lengthening shadows had at last merged into one and the faint after-glow of the red sunset filled the west."

"After nightfall the face of the country seems to alter marvelously, and the clear moonlight only intensifies the change. The river gleams like running quicksilver, and the moonbeams play over the grassy stretches of the plateaus...The Bad Lands seem to be stranger and wilder than ever, the silvery rays turning the country into a kind of grim fairyland."

President Roosevelt had the wherewithal to identify and appreciate the beauty of this great land and to revolt against the losses, waste, corruption, and greed endemic in federal management of natural resources. During a 1907 speech in Memphis, he stated: "As I have said elsewhere, conservation of natural resources is the fundamental problem. Unless we solve that problem it will avail little to solve all others."[6] This was a recurring message throughout his presidency, and he acted upon this concern. His integrity, moral character, and love of nature enabled him to set in motion programs and ideas that reversed the declines.

Roosevelt believed that as President he was steward of the nation's resources. As a fiduciary, the steward is honor bound to husband resources, as he would use his own, for the benefit of the owner - the American people, those alive and those yet to come. Accordingly, he set aside and preserved some 150 million acres of federal land. Much of the land was placed in national forests to provide a constant source of timber and to preserve watersheds. Other land was set aside simply to preserve scenic, historic, or unique qualities for the benefit of all Americans. He also protected land simply to preserve God's creatures, including songbirds "that will perch on the top of a bush or tree and sing for hours in rich, bubbling tones." His diligence as steward preserved untold wealth for over a century.

W. Todd Benson

P.S. To my friend Wade Berryhill, I say, "Read this book, Wade. Aggressive conservationism and environmental protection is something Republicans do, at least the great ones." Sorry the answer took twenty years.

TEDDY ROOSEVELT
A PIONEER CONSERVATIONIST

This is the story of President Theodore Roosevelt's conservation legacy. His legacy is manifested in two forms. One is the philosophy and moral leadership Roosevelt instilled in the federal government - the Executive as steward of public land. Included in this category are the programs he established or strengthened to create national forests, monuments, parks, and refuges. The other part of the Roosevelt legacy is the vast amount of land that he preserved and protected: about 150 million acres of forests, parks, and refuges. This stock has been continually strengthened by subsequent presidents and Congress using the programs, institutions, and leadership that President Roosevelt developed.

Theodore Roosevelt was born in New York City on October 27, 1858. He was brilliant, had an insatiable appetite for natural history, and suffered from asthma. His wealthy parents could afford to school the frail youth at home and this allowed extra opportunity for Roosevelt to pursue, through voracious reading and field exploration, his love of natural science. When still quite young, he resolved to build his body and overcome his asthma. Hiking and exercise went well with his interest in nature. He tramped the woods, hunted, or simply enjoyed the out doors.

He was also schooled in boxing and wrestling, activities he would enjoy throughout much of his life. Forester Gifford Pinchot, who would become Roosevelt's chief of the U.S. Forest Service and close confidant on the environment, did some work for New York while Roosevelt was still governor. He would later recount in his autobiography: "Incidentally, T.R. and I did a little wrestling, at which he beat me; and some boxing, during which I had the honor of knocking the future President of the United States off his very solid pins." [1] Only severe damage to one of Roosevelt's eyes ended boxing at the White House.

Roosevelt attended Harvard from 1876 through 1880 and graduated magna cum laude. After graduation, he returned to New York City, began attending Columbia law school, married Alice Lee, and became a member of the Republican Party. The following year, he was elected to a one-year term in the New York State Assembly (the youngest man ever elected to the Assembly). Two more terms followed and by 1883, he was minority leader. In 1884, his wife Alice died from kidney failure two days after giving birth to their daughter, Alice. On the same day, his mother died from typhoid.

Leaving his new born with his sister, the grief stricken Roosevelt traveled to the Badlands, in what is now Medora, North Dakota, where he recently had purchased two ranches – Chimney Butte and Elkhorn. He remained out west as a rancher through the better part of 1886.

The Badlands, with its "desolate, grim beauty all its own," had a tremendous impact on him. During his time there, he was immersed in the problems of the West and the lives of ordinary, hard-working Americans. He worked and sweated with them. He learned to trust their mettle. "I never would have been President if it had not been for my experiences in North Dakota" he would latter opine. As he explained it to John Burroughs during a train trip through the Badlands on the way to Yellowstone in 1903: "Had he not gone West, he said he never would have raised the Rough Riders Regiment; and had he not raised the regiment and gone to the Cuban War, he would not have been made governor of New York; and had that not happened, the politicians would not unwittingly have made his rise to the Presidency so inevitable."[2]

Politics eventually pulled him back East where, in his own words, he eventually "rose like a rocket" He returned to New York City in 1886 where he unsuccessfully ran for mayor. On December 2, 1886, he married a childhood friend, Edith Carow. They would have five children together. From 1885 through 1889, Roosevelt supplemented his income by writing books: *Hunting Trips of a Ranchman, Life of Thomas Hart Bento, Life of Gouverneur Morris, Ranch Life and the Hunting Trail, Essays in Practical Politics,* and *The Winning of the West.*

Of significance during this time, Roosevelt met George Bird Grinnell, editor of *Forest and Stream* magazine, and the two became good friends. Throughout the remainder of Roosevelt's life, Grinnell strongly influenced Roosevelt on wildlife policy. Grinnell founded the Audubon Society in 1886 to protect non-game birds.[3] In the following year, Grinnell proposed to Roosevelt that they form a club similar to Audubon for the purpose of protecting large game. Roosevelt agreed. In December 1887, Roosevelt hosted a dinner for prospective members and pitched the idea. It was supported and, shortly thereafter, the Boone and Crockett Club was formed. Among the Club's charter provisions was that it work for legislation to protect game and assist in enforcing game laws. In the following years, the Boone and Crockett Club and its members were instrumental in forcing a management policy on Yellowstone Park that ensured true protection of its forests and wildlife. The Club also was instrumental in passage of the 1891 legislation securing to presidents the authority to designate federal forest reserves.

In the 1890s, Roosevelt and Grinnell prepared three books by the Boone and Crockett Club, *American Big-Game Hunting* (1893), *Hunting in Many Lands* (1895), and *Trail and Camp-Fire* (1897). As noted by author John F. Rieger, these books advocated policies that Roosevelt would pursue as president: expansion of national parks and forest reserves, creation of game preserves, and systematic administration of the nation's resources.

Active in the Republican Party, Roosevelt eventually was appointed to the U.S. Civil Service Commission in 1889. Six years later, he was appointed to the New York City Police Board. Shortly thereafter, President McKinley appointed Roosevelt Assistant Secretary of the Navy. In each of these positions, Roosevelt drew attention to himself through his forceful personality and commitment to full and dedicated service. As his eldest daughter, Alice, later recalled, her father had to be the bride at every wedding and the corpse at every funeral. A close friend observed that Roosevelt was not drawn to the limelight, he was the limelight. Or, as John Burroughs put it, the "President himself is something of a storm, - a man of such abounding energy and ceaseless activity that he sets everything in motion around him wherever he goes."[4] By the time war with Spain broke out, Roosevelt was a prominent public figure, particularly in the Northeast and in Republican circles.

When war was declared with Spain, Roosevelt resigned as Assistant Secretary of the Navy and formed the First U.S. Volunteer Cavalry Regiment, a unit that became known as the Rough Riders. He insisted that a professional soldier lead the regiment and Roosevelt began service as second in command. The Rough Riders was a combination of Ivy Leaguers and cowboys. After deployment to Cuba, Roosevelt was promoted from lieutenant colonel to colonel and elevated to command of the Rough Riders. With Roosevelt in command, the Rough Riders played a decisive role in the taking of the San Juan Heights, which brought the end of the very short "splendid little war." Composed of sons from some of the finest families and sustaining the highest casualties of any unit in the war, the Rough Riders dominated news coverage; Roosevelt's name and popularity grew. For his conduct, Roosevelt would be awarded the Congressional Medal of Honor, 100 years later.

Back home, Colonel Roosevelt was a hero. His long public service, party loyalty, and war exploits, along with strong public support, secured for him the Republican nomination for governor of New York. He was elected on November 8, 1898. As governor, Roosevelt advocated environmental policies which were a prelude to his presidency: elimination of patronage in favor of trained professionals, effective reorganization of New York's principal resource agency, vigorous enforcement of existing laws, protection of forests and wildlife, and water quality.[5]

Although loyal to the Republican Party, Roosevelt could not be controlled. He lived by strong moral principles, often an inconvenient trait to fellow politicians. A faction of the New York Republican old guard worked to have Roosevelt selected to run with President McKinley when McKinley ran for his second term. The idea was to bury the increasingly popular Roosevelt in the obscurity of the job of vice president and, more important, get him out of New York. In a letter to one of the plotters, Senator Platt, Roosevelt wrote: "I can't help feeling more and more that the Vice Presidency is not an office in which I could do anything and not an office in which a man is still vigorous and not past middle life has much chance of doing anything. As you know, I am of an active nature. In spite of all the work and all the worry – and very largely because of your own constant courtesy and consideration, my dear Senator – I have thoroughly enjoyed being Governor. ... Certainly everything is being managed now on a perfectly straight basis and every office is clean as a whistle."[6] He continued to protest but the 1900 Republican convention chose Roosevelt.

While McKinley conducted a front porch campaign, vice presidential candidate Roosevelt spent his efforts vigorously campaigning in the West. The McKinley-Roosevelt ticket won a landslide victory. Republican Party boss Senator Mark Hanna was less sanguine about the strategy of "burying" Roosevelt in the vice presidency. Queried Hanna: "Don't any of you realize that there's only one life between this madman and the Presidency?" Hanna's apprehension soon was realized.

At an exposition in Buffalo, New York, September 6, 1901, an anarchist shot McKinley. Vice President Roosevelt, on vacation in Vermont with his family, rushed to McKinley's side. When the doctors announced the President's improvement, a relieved Roosevelt returned to his family, then in New York's Adirondacks. However, McKinley took a turn for the worse and died. On September 14, 1901, Roosevelt was sworn in as President. His fears realized, Senator Hanna exclaimed, "that damned cowboy is President of the United States!"

During the dark days following the assassination, the popular magazine *Century* ran a piece to comfort the nation about the new President. Anonymously written by "An Old Acquaintance," the article said:

> Born of Northern father and Southern mother; commingling in his veins the blood of the English, Dutch, Scotch, and Huguenots; reared in New York, and educated in New England; living a part of his life in the far West, and a part in Washington, where all sections meet on a common plain, Theodore Roosevelt is the most catholic, cosmopolitan, and non-sectional American in public office since Henry Clay.

The article went on to note Roosevelt's "somewhat exuberant enthusiasm" but assured the readers that Roosevelt was "a kind-hearted man, yet a rigid disciplinarian, and will demand faithful and efficient discharge of public duties by public officials."[7] The nation would soon grow to love him.

Throughout his two-term presidency, Roosevelt identified conservation of natural resources as the most pressing problem in America: "As I have said elsewhere, conservation of natural resources is the fundamental problem. Unless we solve that problem it will avail little to solve all others."[8] Indeed, conservation was the first issue that Roosevelt addressed upon assuming the presidency;[9] upon leaving McKinley's funeral, Roosevelt met with Gifford Pinchot and Frederick H. Newell, who would lead Roosevelt's reclamation efforts, to begin planning a national conservation strategy. Conservation was also one of the last issues he addressed; on March 2, 1909, just two days before the inauguration of President Taft, Roosevelt was still protecting land. On March 2, he established the Zuni National Forest and the Mount Olympus National Monument.

In his first message to Congress on December 3, 1901, Roosevelt proclaimed: "The forest and water problems are perhaps the most vital internal problems in the United States."[10] As remembered years later by Pinchot, "Conservation became the characteristic and outstanding policy of T.R's Administration, and has been more generally accepted as such ever since."[11] These are bold comments when one considers that during his two terms of office Roosevelt took on corporate monopolies and trusts, engaged in ending unprecedented labor problems, won the Nobel Peace Prize for resolving the war between Russia and Japan, revitalized the military, settled international disputes involving Venezuela and Costa Rica, revitalized and redefined the Monroe Doctrine, gave America a "square deal," and built the Panama Canal.

At the turn of the 20th century, U.S. policy favored liquidation of real property and natural assets. The Mineral

7

Land Act of 1866 offered free land in exchange for mineral development. The Timber Culture Act of 1873 granted 160 acres to any person who would cultivate timber on 40 acres of the land. The Desert Land Act of 1877 gave arid land at reduced prices to anyone who would irrigate it. The Timber and Stone Act of 1878 allowed land to be sold at discount to promote homesteading. The Homestead Act allowed 160 acres to any one who would homestead.

In the West, federal land was there for the taking. In part, the disposal of resources was driven by the federal government's desire to settle the Midwest and then the West. It also was driven by ignorance and the historically predominant view that the country's assets were inexhaustible.

As of 1901, approximately "one-half of the timber in the United States had been cut, an incalculable amount of precious topsoil had been washed into seas."[12] Thousands of animals were slaughtered for sport and business. "Under the prevailing leasing system, private exploitation of minerals, timber, and water power sites went on apace, even in the so called reserves." [13] Further, under and in violation of the law, grasslands within the forest reserves were "ruthlessly overgrazed."[14] Important historic and archeological sites on federal land were freely open to vandalism, profiteering, and destruction. To exacerbate a bad situation, the U.S. policies provided an environment for abuse and corruption and "great fraud upon the public domain" existed.[15] About this time, John Muir wrote:

> The axe and the saw are insanely busy, chips are flying thick as snowflakes, and every summer thousands of acres of priceless forests, with their underbrush, soil, springs climate, scenery, and religion are vanishing....

All sorts of local laws and regulations have been tried found wanting, and the costly lessons of our experience, as well as that of every civilized nation, show conclusively that the fate of the remnant of our forests is in the hands of the federal government, and that if the remnant is to be saved at all, it must be saved quickly.

Any fool can destroy trees.... It took more than three thousand years to make some of the trees in these Western woods, - trees that are still standing in perfect strength and beauty, waiving and singing in the mighty forests of the Sierra. Through all the wonderful, eventful centuries since Christ's time – and long before that – God has cared for these trees, saved them from drought, disease, avalanches, and a thousand straining, leveling tempests and floods; but he cannot save them from fools, - only Uncle Sam can do that.[16]

Uncle Sam came in the form of President Roosevelt. When Roosevelt assumed the reins of leadership, 560 million federally owned acres in the lower 48 states remained open to entry, exploitation, and settlement.[17] Over the next seven years, Roosevelt would "close" millions of these acres. In the long term, Roosevelt's policies and actions transformed public opinion and governmental policies on federal lands and resources.

Today, federal agencies have different missions for the lands they manage. The National Forest Service is committed to "multiple use" of the nation's forests. The mission of the National Park Service is to conserve the scenery, natural and historic objects, and the wildlife within the national parks and to provide public enjoyment while leaving them unimpaired for future generations. The U.S. Fish and Wildlife Service works to conserve, protect, and enhance fish, plants, and wildlife and their habitat for the benefit of the American people.

During Roosevelt's presidency, the clear lines that distinguished the purpose of national parks, forests, and wildlife refuges did not exist. Indeed, two of the nation's first five parks were actually set aside by Congress as forest reserves – Yosemite and General Grant. Prior to 1897, the secretary of the Department of the Interior (the Department with management authority over forest reserves) closed forest reserves to logging. [18] The first forest reserve, adjacent to Yellowstone National Park, was recommended by Boone and Crockett Club members as a buffer to an expansion of the park. [19]

While some, like Muir, viewed forest reserves as parks, Gifford Pinchot cared little, if at all, about protection of beauty for beauty's sake; Pinchot was for wise use. His thinking on wise use carried through to parks, as well; parks, like forests, were to be used. His favorable attitude about inundating the beautiful Hetch Hetchy Valley in Yosemite National Park in order to provide water and power to San Francisco characteristically demonstrates his philosophy.

Despite uncertainty about the ultimate purposes of parks, reserves, refuges, and other federal holdings, under Roosevelt millions of acres of national lands were no longer relegated to items waiting to be claimed. Rather, Roosevelt's relentless devotion to conservation and preservation resulted in the protection of many of the American treasures enjoyed today.

The tools used by Roosevelt were newly forged or forged during his presidency. In 1891, presidents became authorized to set aside forest reserves, now known as national forests; Roosevelt created 150, encompassing approximately 148 million acres. Also, Congress began the process of setting aside national parks with the establishment of Yellowstone National Park in 1872. The number of parks doubled (from 5 to 10) during his presidency. In 1906, Congress passed the Act for the Preservation of American Antiquities. This act gave the President authority to declare "national monuments" – government owned and protected land identified as possessing prehistoric, historic, or scientific interest. Roosevelt went on to establish 18 national monuments, including the most breathtaking, the Grand Canyon (now a national park).

In addition to the power given to him by Congress, Roosevelt exhibited "an audacious use of executive power."[20] "Is there any law that will prevent me from declaring Pelican Island a Federal Bird Reservation?" Finding there was no such law, he responded: "Very well, then I so declare it."[21] Fifty other bird reservations were to follow. This "can do" attitude was summarized by Roosevelt: "Do what you can with what you have when you can."

Of course, with Teddy Roosevelt, there was always the bully pulpit, which he used to further conservation and preservation. He pressed his message for conservation through high-level conferences, commissions, speeches, publications, and the press.

Throughout his public career, Roosevelt was a master of using the press. According to Stephen Ponder, author of *Managing the Press,* Roosevelt's "promotion of himself and his policies was constant and calculated."[22] Roosevelt not only allowed but and encouraged reporters' access to him. Those who covered him favorably were rewarded with leaks and briefings. Roosevelt similarly courted major magazines. As a result, Roosevelt and his policies were constantly in the forefront of American news.[23]

Roosevelt believed that "properly informing the public was necessary to create support for reform."[24] This philosophy is recognizable, for example, in a letter from Roosevelt to Muir on the issue of Hetch Hetchy: "I will do everything in my power to protect not only the Yosemite, which we already have protected, but other similar great natural beauties of this country. But you must remember that it is out of the question permanently to protect them unless we have a certain degree of friendliness toward them on the part of the people of the State in which they are situated." [25]

Roosevelt recognized that if he could get to the public through the press, he could out maneuver recalcitrant legislative bodies, as he explained in writing about his experience as Governor:

> I had neither the training nor the capacity that would have enabled me to match Mr. Platt[26] and his machine people on their own ground. Nor did I believe that the effort to build up a machine of my own under the then existing conditions would meet the needs of the situation so far as the people were concerned. I therefore made no effort to create a machine of my own, and consistently adopted the plan of going over the heads of the men holding public office and of the men in control of the organization, and appealing directly to the people behind them. ... My success depended upon getting the people in the different districts to look at matters in my way, and getting them to take such an active interest in affairs as to enable them to exercise control over their representatives.[27]

This practice of going over the heads of the politicians drove the New York politicians mad and, in 1901, this madness settled upon Washington.

Roosevelt's efforts in going around the Congress were augmented by Gifford Pinchot's promotion of the Department of Agriculture's Forest Service (Roosevelt's lead agency for forest conservation) and the forest reserves. The Forest Service "sent out a blizzard of mailings to magazines and newspapers, describing the importance of trees and the Forest Service. A novel device for a federal agency, the handouts were widely published. The service also maintained a mailing list of private individuals that by 1909 included some eight hundred thousand names."[28]

Roosevelt also sent numerous messages to Congress. As noted by author Lewis L. Gould, in addition to the eight formal annual messages, Roosevelt would send to Congress approximately four hundred messages. "The technique worked during initial stages of Roosevelt's tenure, but it became an irritant on the Hill during his second term. Lawmakers resented the president's telling them what they must do as well as the public criticism when they failed to act."[29]

Roosevelt also used commissions and conferences to gather information, find experts to verify his agenda, and go around Congress. Again, Gifford Pinchot was a major player in the design and execution of this strategy:

The key to the commission concept was that the President would use his executive authority to appoint agency administrators to a new quasi-presidential body...that would stimulate public discussion of issues stalled in Congress. As the chief investigator of several Roosevelt commissions, Pinchot envisioned a more specific use: generating publicity for conservation through the 'educational' process of public hearings and investigations. The President's involvement made deliberations of the commissions more worth

13

of attention by newspapers and magazines. The resulting news stories also increased the visibility of Roosevelt on the issue popular with many of his reform supporters.[30]

The most notable was the Conference of Governors hosted by Roosevelt on May 13 through 15, 1908. Attendees included governors of the states and territories and members of the cabinet, Congress, and the Supreme Court. Representatives of industry and conservation organizations also attended. In the words of the president, the conference was called "so that we may join together to consider the question of the conservation and use of the great fundamental sources of wealth of this Nation."[31] The conference concluded with a call for future conferences, the creation of conservation commissions in each of the states, and the adoption of laws to enhance conservation.

As a result of the conference, 40 states created conservation commissions.[32] President Roosevelt went on to create the National Conservation Commission. The National Conservation Commission subsequently released an "exhaustive, three-volume report on the state of the nation's natural resources."[33]

A second national conference (the "Second Governors Conference") was convened in December 1908. Twenty governors attended, as did many representatives of the newly formed state conservation commissions. Three months later (February 18, 1909), Roosevelt convened the North American Conservation Commission to address hemispheric conservation issues. This conference recommended that "all nations should be invited to join together in conference on the subject of world resources, and their inventory, conservation, and wise utilization."[34] Roosevelt began preparations for such a conference. The Secretary of State issued invitations on February 19, 1909.

However, the project lapsed when Roosevelt left office in March of that year.[35]

Critics who felt steamrolled by Roosevelt probably did not recognize it, but his use of the bully pulpit was judicious.[36] He was sensitive to the pride and independence of the states and the need for their support. As he explained in a letter to an assistant forest ranger in Santa Barbara, California:

> Would it be possible for you to get up something of a petition that would justify me in saying that there was a genuine movement in the State itself to have the forest rangers made game wardens? I can show you my attitude in the matter the analogy of the Yosemite. I think the Yosemite should be under National control. A lot of good people in California think so too; but until there is strong sentiment – if possible a predominant sentiment – to that effect, I should do damage by advocating it, for I should merely arouse hostility. [37]

The President continued by noting that this approach applied to forest reserves as well. "I want to go just as far in preserving the forests and preserving the game and wild creatures as I can *lead* public sentiment. But if I try to *drive* public sentiment I shall fail, save in exceptional cases."[38] Pinchot was of a similar mind, "Nothing permanent can be accomplished in this country unless it is backed by sound public sentiment."[39]

However, the President sometimes was willing to tackle an issue prior to building a consensus. As he explained, "Occasionally, where I have deemed the case wholly exceptional, I have gone, and in the future in such cases I shall go, directly contrary to public sentiment...; but in a government like ours the wisdom of an extreme step of this kind is directly proportionate to its rarity."[40]

Corruption and mismanagement in the use and transfer of federal lands was a problem. It involved private citizens, corporations, members of the U.S. House of Representatives and the Senate, and members of the Roosevelt administration. As described by Pinchot: "The administration of the public-land laws by the General Land Office of the Interior Department is one of the great scandals of American history. At a time when, in the west, the penalty for stealing a horse was death – death without benefit of law – stealing the public land in open defiance of the law was generally regarded with tolerance or even with approval. It cast no shadow on the reputation of the thief."[41]

Gerald Williams, in his history of the early years of the forest reserve system, presents a rationalization of one land fraud scheme by an attorney. In this particular scheme, an individual would fraudulently files a claim under one of the many statutes for acquiring public land. Upon receipt of title, and the land was promptly conveyed to a business interest. As a participating attorney explained, "nobody is robbed." The citizen filing the fraudulent claim "gets value for the exercise of his right as a citizen; the government gets paid its price for the land, and the land goes to the man or company that sooner or later puts it in use, while the state begins to get annual taxes, which it did not before; so nobody is hurt, but everybody profits, though,…of course perjury may have to be suborned – but that was sanctioned by common usage in land matters."[42]

Beginning in 1903, Roosevelt's administration began to pursue individuals suspected of fraud against the United States. Roosevelt recognized that conservation of national resources could "only be achieved by wise laws and by a resolute enforcement of the laws."[43] As he told Congress in his Third Annual Message: "No man is above the law and no man is below it; nor do we ask any man's permission when we require him to obey it. Obedience to the law is demanded as a right; not asked as a favor." Among other things, Roosevelt prosecuted "every member but one of Oregon's all-Republican congressional delegation."[44]

Indicted Oregon Senator John Mitchell, then 75, "made an impassioned denial of these charges before the Senate, bringing ringing applause from the floor and the galleries."[45] However, the senator was convicted of receiving bribes from land companies. The scandal flowed into other western states, and more prosecutions followed. Before it was over, 100 people were indicted – many of them members of the President's party.

Roosevelt also strove for better management of federal properties. In 1901, management of the national forest reserves was divided among three agencies: The Land Office in the Department of the Interior was charged with management and protection of the reserves; the Geological Survey with surveying the reserves; and the Division of Forestry, within the Department of Agriculture, with technical research.[46] Roosevelt wrote in his autobiography, "the forests were run by clerks in the Division of General Land Office "few if any of whom had ever seen or set foot on the timberlands for which they were responsible. Thus the reserves were neither well protected nor well used."

In 1901, Roosevelt began lobbying for the transfer of the entire reserve program to the Division of Forestry,[47] where Pinchot was in charge. This transfer finally was accomplished on February 1, 1905. With aggressive Pinchot at Forestry's helm, Roosevelt could accelerate his expansion of forest reserves.

The national parks also suffered from divided management. Until the end of his presidency, Roosevelt strove unsuccessfully for consolidated management. This change did come, however, in 1916 with the creation of the National Park Service within the Department of the Interior. Also during Roosevelt's presidency, there was no centralized management of national monuments. Monuments were overseen by the departments of the Interior, Agriculture, and War depending on which department controlled the land when the designation occurred. Consolidated management came later.

Throughout Roosevelt's presidency, protection of public land was always a difficult sell. As noted by Pinchot, "The West wanted development – wanted it at any cost. What helped development was good, and what hindered it was bad. All other concerns came behind that."[48]

Aggressive enforcement of land laws and withdrawal of public lands from the public domain increasingly strained Roosevelt's relationship with many legislators, particularly those in the West. However, use of the bully pulpit and the authority unilaterally to designate refuges, monuments, and forests allowed Roosevelt's conservation agenda to proceed.

One of Roosevelt's last acts was the conveyance to Congress of the report prepared by the First Conference of Governors. In his transmittal remarks, he noted:

> The nation, its government, and its resources exist, first of all, for the American citizen, whatever his creed, race, or birthplace, whether he be rich or poor, educated or ignorant, provided only that he is a good citizen, recognizing his obligations to the nation for the rights and opportunities which he owes to the nation.

Roosevelt's direct actions and moral leadership resulted in the protection of millions of acres of federal land. They include portions of some of our most treasured national areas: Yellowstone, Yosemite, the Grand Canyon, Muir Woods, the Petrified Forest, Sequoia National Forest, Tongas National Forest, and Mesa Verde. During Roosevelt's administration, 150 national forests, five national parks, 51 national bird reservations, four national game preserves, and 18 national monuments were created. These protected lands and the government institutions through which new lands and resources are added and protected are his legacy.

ROOSEVELT'S CONSERVATION PHILOSOPHY

Literature and commentary swirl with discussions about whether Roosevelt was a conservationist or a preservationist. Roosevelt was a conservationist. He believed in the wise use of resources, something we now refer to as sustainable use. But, within his application of wise use was provision for preservation of certain places or things.

Muir is considered a father of the preservation movement, Pinchot a father of conservation. It is not clear that either accolade is correct. As noted by Pinchot biographer Char Miller, Pinchot and Muir historians "have used their subjects to reconstruct the past along certain lines to reaffirm present-day perspectives and values."[49] But, each man was influential and, ultimately, heated rivals over the damming of the Hetch Hetchy Valley during and after the Roosevelt administration. Accordingly, it is beneficial to ask: "What was the difference between Muir and Pinchot and where did Roosevelt stand on these differences?" It appears that there was one salient difference between the two men – Muir found beauty, grace, and God's hand in nature and deemed such wild things worthy of consideration if not protection; Pinchot did not.

"Conservation" was a term used to describe environmental protection as early as 1884 by George Bird Grinnell, editor and publisher of Forest and Stream. Concerning a New York proposal to protect the Adirondack forests from all timber uses, Grinnell stated: "Protection and conservation, now, prompt, adequate – this is what the Adirondack forests demand, not restoration years hence, after the damage from unregulated lumbering shall have been wrought and ruin has followed."[50] Through *Forest and*

Stream and other outlets, Grinnell led campaigns in the 1880s and 1890s to "protect and conserve" the Adirondacks, prohibit the killing of all non-game birds, outlaw market hunting, and secure meaningful protection to Yellowstone national park. The early conservation movement clearly recognized that "wise use" included preservation under the appropriate circumstances.

Nevertheless, Gifford Pinchot claimed credit for inventing "conservation" and he wrote two books about it - The Fight for Conservation and Breaking New Ground. According to Pinchot, he was struck by an inspirational thunderbolt while riding his horse in 1907. At that time, he realized that his methods for forest policy should be extended to all government resources under the title "conservation." Thereafter, he fervently proselytized on behalf of "conservation." His doctrine reached its zenith at the President's 1908 Governor's Conference and a brief time immediately thereafter, although the Pinchot definition had a solid home for many years in the U.S. Forest Service.[51] His definition of "conservation" (which is really a collage of principles) profoundly influenced public debate and the programs and policies of the U.S. Forest Service.

According to Pinchot: "The conservation issue is a moral issue, and the heart of it is this: For whose benefit shall our natural resources be conserved – for the benefit of us all, or for the use and profit of a few? This truth is so obvious and the question itself so simple that the attitude toward conservation of any man in public or private life indicates his stand in the fight for public rights."[52]

"The first great fact about conservation is that it stands for development. There has been a fundamental misconception that conservation means nothing more than the husbanding of resources for future generations. There could be no more serious mistake. Conservation does mean provision for the future, but it means also and first of all the recognition of the right of the present generation to the fullest necessary use of all the resources with which this country is so abundantly blessed. Conservation demands the welfare of this generation first, and afterward the welfare of the generation to follow."[53] Pinchot further defined conservation as the prevention of waste, the development and preservation of natural resources for the benefit of the many, not merely the benefit of the few, and the greatest good to the greatest number for the longest time.[54] Pinchot concluded that "[c]onservation advocates the use of foresight, prudence, thrift, and intelligence in dealing with public matters ....It proclaims the right and duty of the people to act for the benefit of the people."[55]

This is good stuff! Who could be against conservation?[56] "Conservation" recognized that public lands belong to all of the people and are held in trust for the common good. "Conservation" abhorred waste, monopoly, and profiteering at the public expense. It was practical, useful, and necessary for the times. Pinchot's "conservation" permitted the significant slowing of plunder and pillage of federal lands. As one historian noted, were it not for Pinchot's aggressive implementation of conservation of national forests, we would only have stumps and washed-out soil to argue about today. Pinchot cleared the way to allow Roosevelt his great environmental legacy.

Pinchot's universal formula, however useful and necessary, had a major limitation. As strange as it may sound today, Pinchot's formula was limited to economic considerations; the magnificence of nature and all its glory had no value unless it could be quantified and weighed and measured against man's needs. Consider, Pinchot's dismissive journal entry in 1913 subsequent to congressional hearings on the damming of a portion of Yosemite National Park – "Opposition reduced mainly to 'nature-lovers.'"[57] The "fullest use" advocated by Pinchot meant development; nothing was to be spared.

There is no corresponding disciple who sets forth the parameters of "preservation"[58] as fully as Pinchot delineates "conservation." We simply know that "preservationism" is something else than what Pinchot advocated and that the concept of "preservation" is embodied in the words and deeds of John Muir. But, the assertion that Muir was not Pinchot does not directly tell us what is meant by "preservation."

Pinchot (and conservation) abhorred waste. Certainly, Muir did not favor waste; he, too, opposed it. This is brought home wonderfully well in Our National Parks[59] in which Muir castigates the waste of resources, in particular trees, by the railroad and mining interests, the harvesters of redwoods, and the "happy robbers," the shake makers.

Pinchot supported the use of resources to benefit the many rather than the few. So did Muir. Muir encouraged use of the forests. Muir encouraged tourism within the national parks. Indeed, one of the charter purposes of the Sierra Club in 1892 was to promote access to the Sierra Nevada Mountains, including Yosemite.[60] Subsequent to the western tour of the nation's forest reserves by the Forestry Commission in 1896, Muir published a series of articles designed to influence Congress and public opinion on forest reserve policy. These articles subsequently were published in a 1901 book titled Our National Parks. In it, Muir said:

> Surely, then, it should not be wondered at that lovers of their country, bewailing its baldness, are now crying aloud, "Save what is left of the forests!" Clearing has surely now gone far enough; soon timber will be scarce and not a grove will be left to rest or pray in. The remnant protected will yield plenty of timber, a perennial harvest for every right use, without further diminution of its area, and will continue to cover the springs of the rivers

that rise in the mountains and give irrigating waters to the dry valleys at their feet, prevent wasting floods, and be a blessing to everybody forever.[61]

Continuing, Muir cited Prussia's forests as a model for the United States: "But the state woodlands are not allowed to lie idle. On the contrary, they are made to produce as much timber as possible without spoiling them. In the administration of its forests, the state righteously considers itself bound to treat them as a trust for the nation as a whole, and to keep in view the common good of the people for all time."[62]

Muir's language is classic Pinchot, with one exception; there are no indications in Pinchot's work during his years as a U.S. Forester suggesting Pinchot would mourn the loss of a grove to "pray in."[63] As noted earlier, this is the salient difference between Muir and Pinchot. Muir recognized the beauty in every blade of grass or gust of wind and that the magnificence of nature had to be a factor in any discussion of its fate.

Consider, for example, Pinchot's and Muir's view of forests. Pinchot states:

Full utilization of the productive power of the Forests…does not take place until after the land has been cut over in accordance with the rules of scientific forestry. The transformation from a wild to a cultivated forest must be brought about by the ax. Hence, the importance of substituting as fast as practicable, the actual use for the mere hoarding of timber.[64]

We are told that while Pinchot was studying forestry in France, he was impressed by the way French forests "were divided at regular intervals by perfectly straight paths and roads at right angles to each other."[65] Conversely, Muir finds that "[n]one of Nature's landscapes are ugly so long as they are wild...."[66] Compare further one on Muir's many descriptions of Yosemite:

> Hazel Green is a good place quietly to camp and study, to get acquainted with the trees and birds, to drink the reviving water and weather, and to watch the changing lights of the big charmed days. The rose light of the dawn, creeping higher among the stars, changes to daffodil yellow; then come the level enthusiastic sunbeams pouring across the feathery ridges, touching pine after pine, spruce and fir, libocedrus and lordly sequoia, searching every recess, until all are awakened and warmed.[67]

President Roosevelt obviously supported, implemented, and championed "conservation." As he noted more than once: "Conservation means development as much as it does protection. I recognize the right and duty of this generation to develop and use the natural resources of our land; but I do not recognize the right to waste them, or to rob, by wasteful use, the generations that come after us."[68] However, Roosevelt, like Grinnell and Muir, knew that special things worthy of protection resided in nature.

While he was a member of the New York Assembly, Roosevelt worked to create the Adirondack State Forest Preserve.[69] Pinchot did not approve:

> In 1885 New York State created the Adirondack State Forest Preserve, not for Forestry, but to "preserve" the forest and the water supply. The exclusion of Forestry from the Preserve was made certain, in 1891, by an

amendment to the State Constitution which forbade the cutting of any tree. That indefensible provision is still in force.[70]

Within a month of becoming President under tumultuous circumstances, Roosevelt had already asked his Attorney General whether he could use forest reserves to protect wildlife. Attorney General Knox, in an opinion letter dated November 29, 1901, informed the President that "it has long been the policy to permit free access [to public land] for any and all purposes not violative of law, and especially (except as otherwise provided in special cases) for the purpose of hunting, trapping, and fishing." The answer was no, only Congress could alter long established policy. Roosevelt immediately asked the Congress to rectify this shortcoming in the law in his first State of the Union Address Roosevelt one month later; he argued that forestry policy should do more than protect wood and water:

> Some at least of the forest reserves should afford perpetual protection to native fauna and flora, safe harbor of refuge to our rapidly diminishing wildlife wild animals of the large kind, and free camping grounds for the ever increasing members of men and women who have learned to find rest, health, and recreation in the splendid forests and flower-clad meadows of our mountains.

In a 1903 speech in Sacramento after returning from a camping trip in Yosemite, Roosevelt distinguished between preservation for wise use and preservation for aesthetic and spiritual values. He recognized the need for both, depending upon circumstances. Speaking to the spiritual values of nature, Roosevelt stated: "Lying out at night under those giant sequoias was lying in a temple built by no hand of man, a temple grander than any human architect could by any possibility build, and I hope for the preservation of the groves of giant trees simply because it would be a shame to our civilization to let them disappear. They are monuments in themselves." [71]

In a book he published in 1905, President Roosevelt observed:

> There can be nothing in the world more beautiful than the Yosemite, the groves of the giant sequoias and redwoods, the Canyon of the Colorado, the Canyon of the Yellowstone, and the Three Tetons; and our people should see to it that they are preserved for their children and their children's children forever, with their majestic beauty all unmarred. [72]

Roosevelt continued to look for ways to achieve his ends. Congress was asked to amend the forestry laws. Congress was asked to create wildlife refuges and establish and improve hunting laws. Roosevelt further worked to gain public support for parks and other forms of preservation. He dispatched armed forces to stop poaching on Midway and in Alaska. And, early in his presidency (March 14, 1903), Roosevelt simply ignored his Attorney General's prior advice and began designating bird reservations, principally for the benefit of non-game species. "Is there any law that will prohibit me from declaring Pelican Island a national bird preserve?" Roosevelt asked his Attorney General. Hearing there was none, Roosevelt responded, "Very well, then - I so declare it." [73]

In his last State of the Union Address, President Roosevelt noted that "Yellowstone Park....like the Yosemite, is a great wonderland, and should be kept as a national playground. In both, all wild things should be protected and the scenery kept wholly unmarred."

27

Roosevelt's efforts and desires for preservation were known to his friends and colleagues, as evidenced by George Bird Grinnell's tribute to Roosevelt in the introduction to *American Big Game in its Haunts; The Book of the Boone and Crockett Club* published in 1904:

It is not too much to say, however, that the chair of chief magistrate has never been occupied by a sportsman whose range of interests was so wide, and so actively manifested, as in the case of Mr. Roosevelt. It is true that Mr. Harrison, Mr. Cleveland, and Mr. McKinley did much in the way of setting aside forest reservations, but chiefly from economic motives; because they believed that forests should be preserved both for the timber that they might yield, if wisely exploited, and for their value as storage reservoirs for the waters of our rivers.

The view taken by Mr. Roosevelt is quite different. To him, the economics of the case appeal with the same force that they might have for the hard-headed, common sense business American; but beyond this, and perhaps, if the secrets of his heart were known, more than this, Mr. Roosevelt is influenced by a love of nature, which, though considered sentimental by some, is, in fact, nothing more than far-sightedness, which looks toward the health, happiness, and general well-being of the American race for the future.[74]

Roosevelt confirmed Grinnell's assessment of him in a subsequent chapter on wilderness reserves. While acknowledging the economic role of the forest reserve system,[75] Roosevelt stated that "it is wise, here and there to keep selected portions of it ... in a state of nature ... for the sake of preserving all its beauties and wonders unspoiled by greedy and shortsighted vandalism."[76] Continuing, Roosevelt stated:

> The wild creatures of the wilderness add to it by their presence a charm which it can acquire in no other way. On every ground it is well for our nation to preserve, not only for the sake of this generation, but above all for the sake of those who come after us, representatives of the stately and beautiful haunters of the wilds which were once found throughout our great forests, over the vast lonely plains, and on the high mountain ranges, but which are now on the point of vanishing save where they are protected in natural breeding grounds and nurseries. The work of preservation must be carried on in such a way as to make it evident that we are working in the interests of the people as a whole, not in the interest of any particular class; and that the people benefited beyond all others are those who dwell nearest to the regions in which the reserves are placed. The movement for the preservation by the nation of sections of the wilderness as national playgrounds is essentially a democratic movement in the interest of all our people.[77]

In 1912, Roosevelt was on the editorial board of The Outlook, a weekly magazine. On February 3, 1912, The Outlook editorially supported the establishment of a National Park Service citing, in part, "the value of beauty as a National asset."[78] The Outlook further supported the re-adoption of a law limiting water withdrawals from the Niagara River. Among the reasons cited were that: (1) the American people have determined that the Niagara Falls

29

should be preserved as a precious National possession; (2) preserving Niagara is a national duty; and (3) the scenic beauty of Niagara Falls has suffered from prior withdrawals and further injury should not be allowed.[79] This is not Pinchot conservatism. It is the next step beyond Pinchot; it is recognition that nature has intangible benefits that strengthen us individually and collectively as a nation and that the beauty of nature must be preserved.

Pinchot's aggressive application of forestry and the free reign that Roosevelt gave him were necessary to slow the incredible destruction to and waste of the nation's forests and associated resources. Pinchot's devotion to economic forestry was absolutely necessary in order to engender public and legislative support and it was required by the forestry laws. Roosevelt trusted and backed Pinchot. Roosevelt believed in and promoted economic forestry and resource development.

But, Roosevelt, like Muir, recognized that sometimes more was required. Accordingly, Roosevelt worked to expand the public debate and, more importantly, the preserved areas and wildlife of the nation. As Roosevelt noted "to lose the chance to see frigatebirds soaring in circles above the storm, or a file of pelicans winging their way homeward across the crimson afterglow of the sunset, or a myriad terns flashing in the bright light of midday as they hover in a shifting maze above the beach – why, the loss is like the loss of a gallery of the masterpieces of the artists of old time."[80] Roosevelt was not prepared to allow such loss.

THE FIRST TERM
1901 - 1905

In September 1901, Vice President Roosevelt was hiking in the Adirondacks. During a lunch break, he noticed a lone hiker moving rapidly up the path. The runner bore the message that President McKinley was in grave condition. For the second time in a week, Roosevelt rushed to the president. He arrived too late. On September 14, Theodore Roosevelt was sworn in as President.

President Roosevelt was an energetic man of great confidence and conviction. Only 42, the youngest to serve as President, and only three months in office, he prepared his first "annual message" to Congress.[81] It was transmitted to Congress on December 3, 1901. Contained within his message were themes he would return to again and again throughout his presidency: forest and water conservation, reclamation, wildlife protection, land reform, and government reform.

A principal component of his first message was the need for wise use of the nation's resources: "Wise forest protection does not mean the withdrawal of forest resources, whether wood, water, or grass, from contributing their full share to the welfare of the people, but, on the contrary gives the assurance of larger and more certain supplies. The fundamental idea of forestry is the perpetuation of forests by use. Forest protection is not an end of itself; it is a means to increase and sustain the resources of our country and the industries that depend upon them."

To emphasize this point, Roosevelt focused on the utility of forests, noting that they are essential for business. Whatever destroys the forests, unless it is agriculture, he asserted, threatens to destroy the country. Accordingly, Roosevelt declared, "[a]dditions should be made [to the forest reserves] whenever practicable, and their usefulness should be increased by a thoroughly business-like management."

Roosevelt also stressed the role of forests in maintaining the health and stability of ecosystems. "The forests are natural reservoirs. By restraining the streams in flood and replenishing them in drought, they make possible the use of the waters otherwise wasted. They prevent the soil from washing, and so protect the storage reservoirs from filling up with silt. Forest conservation is therefore an essential condition of water conservation."

Not only were forests to be managed for trees or used to secure the nation's water, Roosevelt also called for them needed to be set aside "as preserves for the wild forest creatures." Shortly after becoming president, Roosevelt asked his Attorney General if the forest reserve Organic Act authorized the Secretary of the Interior to set aside portions of the forest reserves as wildlife sanctuaries. If not, he asked whether mere ownership by the federal government authorized regulatory control.

In his ruling, Attorney General Knox stated that "from the beginning, it has been the policy to permit access for any and all purposes not violative of the law, and especially...for the purpose of hunting, trapping, and fishing." Continuing, he said that "the Secretary of the Interior can not, without express authority of law, change this long-settled policy of the Government...by rules or regulations." He concluded, "[u]nder these circumstances, I am constrained to the opinion that, until further legislation, the Secretary of the Interior is not authorized to prescribe rules and regulations by which the national forest reserves may be made refuges for game, or which the hunting, killing or capture of game in such reserves is forbidden." This negative response prompted the president's December 3 supplication to Congress for legislation authorizing the use of forest reserves as wildlife sanctuaries.[82]

In his State of the Union address, Roosevelt further identified the need for more efficient government to protect and manage the forest reserves. "The present diffusion of responsibility is bad from every standpoint," the President declared. Among other things, he noted, the situation "prevents the effective co-operation between the Government and the men who utilize the resources of the reserves, without which the interests of both must suffer."

Roosevelt requested Congress to consolidated these responsibilities within the Department of Agriculture. Finally, the President addressed the issue of reclamation. This topic had two broad purposes. The first was to establish reservoirs that could take advantage of floods and freshets by storing surplus water. The second was to take surplus water and distribute it among arid lands. Roosevelt identified reclamation as the province of the federal government. In his opinion, the resources of private interests and the individual states were inadequate to properly handle the job. Moreover, far-reaching, interstate issues and problems were encompassed in the issue of reclamation; national problems required national planning and solutions.

In response to the President's call for consolidation of the forests under the Department of Agriculture, Congressman John F. Lacey introduced legislation for the transfer. On March 15, Congressman Lacey's bill was approved by the Public Lands Committee and went to the full House, where many opposed it.

Significant Western sentiment was that the forest reserve system was a means of creating wilderness playgrounds for rich easterners. The West wanted no part of it. Years later, Gifford Pinchot, the principal architect of and spokesman for Congressman Lacey's bill, cited Congressman Bell's comments as representative of the opposition: "Bell of Colorado declared that the people of his state wanted no buffalo pastures and hunting preserves for rich Easterners."[83] Bell further claimed that the "sole purpose of the bill was to build up a lot of English game preserves."[84] The Lacey bill went down to defeat, 100 to 73. One hundred and fifty-nine Congressmen abstained, and 19 voted present. Moreover, Roosevelt soon learned that the fight was not over. Throughout the year new bills were introduced that were intended, in part, to weaken the forest reserve system. All were defeated. As noted by Pinchot in his autobiography, during 1902 the "whole Forest Reserve policy was still in jeopardy. That year, and for several years to follow, it was in fact less a question of securing good legislation than of preventing bad. The danger was often so acute that the Reserves were saved only by the skin of their teeth. Over and over again their escape seemed almost miraculous."[85]

Roosevelt suffered another setback with the defeat of the Lacy Bill. It contained a provision authorizing the President to establish wildlife sanctuaries within forest reserves if governors requested them. The Congress did, however, pass an Alaskan Game Act which regulated hunting and prohibited the export of certain wildlife out of Alaska.

Throughout 1902, his first full year as President, Roosevelt made modest advances in his conservation agenda. Thirteen forest reserves were established – Alaska's 4.5 million acre Alexander Archipelago Forest Reserve, Arizona's Chiricahua, Mount Graham, Santa Catalina, and Santa Rita Forest Reserves, San Isabel Forest Reserve in Colorado, Absaroka, Little Belt and Madison Forest Reserves in Montana, Dismal River and Niobarra Forest Reserves in Nebraska, and the Lincoln Forest Reserve in New Mexico, more than 10.5 million acres. Also, the

Newlands Reclamation Act became law, providing a source of funding for reclamation projects through the sale of public lands in 13 western states and three territories.

During the difficult year of 1902, a jewel was added to the U.S. system of parks – Crater Lake, a brilliant blue lake. Congressman Thomas Tounge introduced legislation in 1898 and 1899 for the creation of Crater Lake National Park. Both bills failed to pass.[86] A new bill, supported by Roosevelt, was introduced. The speaker of the House refused to allow the bill to come to a vote. Roosevelt interceded, the speaker relented, and the bill passed. The President signed the law creating Crater Lake National Park May 22, 1902.

Unlike designations of forest reserves and, subsequently, national monuments, no comprehensive act existed for national parks. The purpose of each was set case-by-case. Crater Lake was "set apart as a public park or pleasuring ground for the benefit of the people." Timber harvest and development were prohibited; the federal administration was charged with making rules to preserve the natural objects within the park and protect the fish and game from wanton destruction.

Roosevelt began his environmental comments in his Second Annual Message to Congress complimenting the Congress for passing of the Newlands Reclamation Bill and its commitment to irrigate the arid West. Roosevelt then pushed the forest reserve portion of his agenda: "Now that this policy of national irrigation has been adopted, the need of through and scientific forest protection will grow more rapidly than ever throughout the public land states."

Roosevelt renewed his request for federal protection of game. "Legislation should be provided for the protection of the game, and the wild creatures generally, on the forest reserves. The senseless slaughter of game, which can by judicious protection be permanently preserved on our national reserves for the people as a whole, should be stopped at once."

Alaska also warranted the President's attention. In addition to general management issues concerning this enormous territory, Roosevelt urged Congress to take action necessary to protect and preserve Alaska's forests, game, and salmon fisheries.

The President warned Congress about abuses under laws designed to foster homesteading but which were perverted to allow acquisition of large tracts of public land. As part of his report, Roosevelt introduced a concept that would become one of the hallmarks of his presidency: a commission of experts to report on designated issues. In this case, Roosevelt recommended that Congress appoint a commission to study and report upon the use and condition of public lands.

In 1903, Roosevelt established nearly a dozen forest reserves and signed legislation creating Wind Cave National Park in the Black Hills of South Dakota. Wind Cave is one of the longest and most complex caves in the world.

The President became increasingly alarmed by the destruction of birds, principally through the millenary trade. In 1900, while governor of New York, Roosevelt signed legislation sponsored by the New York Audubon Society to restrict hunting. Birds, he wrote, "add immeasurably to the wholesome beauty of life."[87] As President, he was receptive when representatives of the Florida Audubon Society pressed him for a bird sanctuary at Pelican Island – federal land on Florida's east coast. Thwarted by his prior inquiry to the Attorney General concerning his authority to regulate federal land to protect wildlife and his two requests to Congress for appropriate legislation, he rephrased the question to his Attorney General: "Is there any law that prevents me from declaring a bird reservation?" Hearing that there was no such law, he acted; on March 14, what is today Pelican Island National Wildlife Refuge was established. Fifty more designations by executive order would follow, establishing the nucleus of today's spectacular National Wildlife Refuge system.

On April 1, Roosevelt left for an extended trip through the West. Along with one of America's greatest naturalists and nature writers, John Burroughs, he traveled by train through the Badlands and to Yellowstone National Park. For two weeks, he rode, hiked, skied, snow-shoed, and camped throughout the majestic park. He and Burroughs parted company and the Roosevelt proceeded on a long sweep of the Plains, Southwest, and Rocky Mountain states. This trip took him to the Grand Canyon on May 6.

The Grand Canyon had a profound impact on him. While there, he implored the people of Arizona to "not have a building of any kind, not a summer cottage, a hotel, or anything else, to mar the wonderful grandeur, sublimity, the great loneliness and beauty of the cañon." Writing to his daughter Ethel on May 10, 1903, he stated:

> It was very interesting going through New Mexico and seeing the strange old civilization of the desert, and the next day the Grand Cañon of Arizona, wonderful and beautiful beyond description. I could have sat and looked at it for days. It is a tremendous chasm, a mile deep and several miles wide, the cliffs carved into battlements, amphitheaters, towers, and pinnacles, and the coloring wonderful, red and yellow and gray and green.[88]

In 1905, he again expressed his feelings in a book entitled *Outdoor Pastimes of an American Hunter*: "It is hard to make comparisons among different kinds of scenery, all of them very grand and beautiful; but nothing I have seen has impressed me quite as much as the desolate and awful sublimity of the Grand Cañon of the Colorado. I earnestly wish that Congress would make it a national park...."[89]

Roosevelt then traveled to Yosemite. At his request, John Muir acted as his guide.

When the President arrived at Yosemite, politicians, bureaucrats, courtiers, and lobbyists who sought to fete him at a local lodge. However, Roosevelt came to see Yosemite with Muir, and see it with Muir he would. Along with a cook and packer, Muir and Roosevelt slipped into the mountains and woods. Roosevelt described the trip in his autobiography: "The first night was clear, and we lay down in the darkening aisles of the great Sequoia grove. The majestic trunks, beautiful in color and in symmetry, rose round us like pillars of a mightier cathedral than ever was conceived even by the fervor of the Middle Ages. ... The second night we camped in a snow-storm, on the edge of the cañon walls under the spreading limbs of a grove of mighty silver fir; and the next day we went down into the wonderland of the valley itself. I shall always be glad I was in the Yosemite with John Muir...."[90]

For two days and nights, Muir and Roosevelt rode, hiked, camped, and bonded. The third day called for a trip through the Yosemite Valley. Roosevelt stopped at the lodge long enough to pay his respects to the crowd still waiting to fete him. He passed up a banquet and entertainment, including a spotlight show on the valley walls, and traveled up the valley with Muir and made camp for the night.

Each developed a respect for the other. Noted Muir: "I never before had such had so interesting, hearty, and manly a companion. I fairly fell in love with him." [91]

Although their paths never again crossed, they exchanged letters and remained friends until Muir's death in 1914. Muir thereafter kept a picture of Roosevelt on the wall of his study.[92]

Congress failed to act on Roosevelt's request in his annual message for a public lands commission. Accordingly, the President appointed his own. The commission documented widespread fraud. Some was bribery to expedite illegal patents. False claims would be filed and when title passed to the homesteader, he would immediately convey it to a business interest. In timber rich Minnesota, nine of 10 claims were passed through to businesses; in mining areas, almost all were. Much fraud occurred under the Forest Lieu Land provisions of the 1897 Organic Act, which allowed landowners within a reserve to swap their property for federal land outside it. The defrauders, through bribery, would identify pending forest reserves. Then, they would claim worthless land within the prospective reserve. Once the reserve was established, they would swap it for land many times its value which could be sold at exorbitant profit. Other times, public land was illegally fenced and appropriated to private use.

December 7, 1903, brought Roosevelt back to Congress with his Third Annual Message. His began his environmental comments with a discussion of Alaska, requesting land laws and surveys necessary to protect Alaska's resources. Roosevelt stressed anew his belief in wise use: "The fisheries, if wisely handled and kept under national control, will be a business as permanent as any other, and of utmost importance to the people. The forests, if properly guarded will form another great source of wealth."

Roosevelt again renewed and emphasized his concern over the implementation of public land laws. In his opinion, the laws were not encouraging settlement, they were simply allowing a few to amass large holdings. He requested legislation designed to withhold federal land for all purposes except settlement.

He further used his address to inform Congress about how he intended to proceed with reform:

> I have appointed a commission composed of W.A. Richlands, Commissioner of the General Land Office; Gifford Pinchot, Chief of the Bureau of Forestry of the Department of Agriculture, and F. H. Newell, Chief Hydrographer of the Geological Survey, to report at the earliest practical moment upon the condition, disposal, and settlement of the public lands. The commission will report especially what changes in organization, laws, regulations, and practice affecting the public lands are needed to effect the largest practicable disposition of the public lands to actual settlers who will build permanent homes upon them, and to secure in permanence the fullest and most effective use of the resources of the public lands.

Government reform was again laid before Congress: "The administrative features of forest reserves are at present unsatisfactory, being divided between three Bureaus of two Departments." Again, Congress was asked to consolidate forest reserve responsibilities within the Department of Agriculture. He argued that the complaints over the forest reserves were due to ineffective management, not the reserves themselves. "Fix the mismanagement and all would prosper."

The year 1904 saw modest advancement of Roosevelt's conservation agenda. Several forest reserves were established. The President also established his second national bird reserve: Breton Island, Louisiana.

In 1904, Congress passed an act modifying a land agreement with the Sisseton, Wahpeton, and Cut Head bands of the Sioux tribe located on the Devils Lake Reservation. As part of that act, Congress set aside 900 acres and authorized Roosevelt to establish a public park there. He exercised this authority on June 2, 1904 by creating the Sully's Hill National Park. In 1914, Sully's Hill was designated Sully's Hill National Game Preserve. Today, Sulley's Hill maintains herds of bison and elk.

Roosevelt's 1904 election as President was a decisive victory. He won every region except for the South. On election night, he declared that he considered this to be a second term and, in the tradition of presidents before him, would not seek another term. Thereafter, Roosevelt's conservation initiatives escalated.

One month after the election, Roosevelt was again before Congress with his Fourth Annual Message. Speaking of forests, he acknowledged prior "misunderstanding and complaint" - a great understatement given Pinchot's observation that during the first years the entire forest reserve system escaped by the skin of its teeth. Buoyed by his success at the polls, Roosevelt began a new offensive to reform the forest reserve system. He started with a detailed recitation of the purposes of the reserves - to preserve water and lumber supply. He reasserted his position that the "cardinal principle of the forest-reserve policy…[is] that the reserves are for use. Whatever interferes with the use of their resources is to be avoided by every possible means. But the…resources must be used in such a way as to make them permanent." He emphasized his refusal to be influenced by those whose only interest in the forests was temporary, those who cut the forests and moved on.

Roosevelt also used the prior complaints to again urge consolidation of forest administration. "The present arrangement is bad at every point of view. Merely to mention it is to prove it must be terminated at once." He pointed to the support of his proposal by major users of western lands, the National Livestock Association, the American Mining Congress, the National Wool Growers Association, the National Irrigation Congress, and the National Board of Trade. In an attempt to shame Congress, Roosevelt emphasized that nearly all of the great nations consolidated their forest services as he had.

Finally, he again explained the expected benefits from consolidation: a better handling of forest work because it would be under a single, experienced entity; better service to the people in the west because services and decision making would occur at local offices; and forest reserves would become self-supporting. As to forest reserves, Roosevelt concluded:

> Every administrative officer concerned is convinced of the necessity for the proposed consolidation of forest work in the Department of Agriculture, and I myself have urged it more than once in former messages. Again I commend it to the early and favorable consideration of the Congress. The interests of the Nation at large and of the West in particular have suffered greatly' strongest preservation message to date.

He again reminded Congress of the need for wildlife refuges. He urged the Congress to invest him with the authority to set aside portions of forest reserves or other public lands for the preservation of the bison, the wapti, and other large beasts once so abundant in our woods and mountains and our great plains, and now tending toward extinction. "We owe it to future generations," he explained, "to keep alive and beautiful creatures which by their presence add such distinctive character to the American wilderness."

Part of his message to Congress also called for the expansion of Yellowstone National Park and the creation of similar parks at the Grand Canyon and at Yosemite. The Yosemite request included the recommendation that Congress place include "as many as possible of the of the groves of giant trees in California."

In January, Gifford Pinchot convened a meeting of forest users in Washington state. Representatives of Western lumber, railroads, and livestock, and small cattle interests attended. The consensus was that the administration's "wise-use" approach was in their interest and they determined to back the president's call for transfer of the forest reserves to the Department of Agriculture.[93]

Congress finally reacted favorably.

In January, a bill was presented to Roosevelt establishing the Wichita Game Preserve. The president signed the legislation on January 24, 1905. When established, the preserve was bereft of buffalo. Restocking first occurred in 1907 after Congress appropriated money to fence a major portion of the preserve. The New York Zoological Society donated the first 15 bison. Today, herds of bison, elk, deer, and long-horned cattle are preserved on Wichita's 59,000 acres.

The significant difference between Wichita, established by Congress, and the bird reservations established unilaterally by executive order, was money. Then, as now, Congress controlled it. For Wichita, money was appropriated paying for fencing and park maintenance. The bird reservations were protected only by the force of the moral force of the president's designation or the game wardens hired through contributions.

Despite little funding, the bird reservations succeeded. Roosevelt had the occasion to discuss Passage

Key Bird Reservation in 1916, nine years after he established it. In the book, *A Book-Lover's Holidays in the Open*, Roosevelt observed:

> [M]uch has been accomplished. This particular reservation [Passage Key National Wildlife Refuge] was set apart by presidential proclamation in 1905. Captain Sprinkle was at once put in charge. Of the five chief birds, the royal terns, Caspian terns, Cabot's terns, laughing gulls, and skimmers, there were that season about one thousand nests. This season, ten years later, there are about thirty-five thousand nests. The brown pelicans and Louisiana herons also show a marked increase. The least tern, which had been completely exterminated or driven away, has returned and is breeding in fair numbers.[94]

Before the end of his first term, Congress presented the president with more requested legislation. First came the Forest Transfer Act, transferring administration of the forest reserves to the Department of Agriculture. Similar to the funding mechanism in the Newlands Reclamation Act, money from the sale of forest lands and timber was allocated for forest improvement and management. This legislation was signed on February 1, 1905. By March 3, national park and forest bureau employees were given law enforcement authority. Shortly thereafter, they also were given the authority of game wardens.

Of particular significance, the Transfer Act made Forest Bureau employees part of the civil service. Until then, forest rangers and superintendents were political appointees named after consultation with Senators from the host states, inviting the massive fraud.

In announcing the transfer of forest reserves and employees from the Department of the Interior to the Forest Bureau within the Department of Agriculture, the Secretary of Agriculture stated to Forest Bureau Chief Gifford Pinchot:

In the administration of the forest reserves it must be borne in mind that all land is to be devoted to the most productive use for the permanent good of the whole people and not for the temporary benefit of individuals or companies. All of the resources of forest reserves are for use, and this must be brought about in a thoroughly prompt and businesslike manner, under such restrictions only as will insure permanence of these resources....You will see to it that water, wood, and forage of the reserves are conserved and wisely used for the benefit of the home-builder first of all, upon whom depends the best permanent use of lands and resources alike.[95]

As part of his new authority and with Roosevelt's support, Gifford Pinchot initiated a fee for grazing on public lands. In a letter to Pinchot, Roosevelt reminded him of the severe damage brought about because of the open range. The President concluded:

It must not be forgotten that the forest reserves belong to all the people, but the grazing privilege can be used only by a few. It is therefore only just and right that those who enjoy the special advantages of a protected range should contribute the expense of handling the reserves.

Important progress has been made in the forest reserves in the practical solution of the grazing problems, and I heartily approve the general policy outlined in the new rules and regulations.[96]

Ultimately the grazing fee was challenged in court. It was not until after Pinchot left office that the grazing fee regulations were upheld by the United States Supreme Court in *U.S. v. Grimurd.* The court declared that the Department of Agriculture "is required to make provision to protect...[the forest reserves] from depredations and harmful uses." Accordingly, it is "authorized to 'regulate the occupancy and use and to preserve the forests from destruction.'"[97]

On March 4, 1905, President Roosevelt was sworn in for a second term in office.

THE SECOND TERM
1905 – 1909

In 1905, Roosevelt established or reorganized some 40 new forest reserves and four new bird reservations: Stump Lake, North Dakota; Siskiwit Islands, Michigan; Passage Key, Florida; and Huron Islands, Michigan.

Roosevelt also wrote *Outdoor Pastimes of an American Hunter,* published in October. The vignettes, principally from Roosevelt's trips west, include the 1903 trip to Yellowstone, Yosemite, and the Grand Canyon and a hunting trip for wolves and bear in Oklahoma and Colorado in April and May in 1905. A third trip, taken by Vice President-elect Roosevelt to hunt cougar in Colorado, is chronicled as well as hunting stories from his earlier life in North Dakota. The chapters are indicative of the subject and include With the Cougar Hounds, A Colorado Bear Hunt, Wolf-Coursing, Hunting in the Cattle Country – The Prongbuck, A Shot at a Mountain Sheep, The Whitetail Deer, The Mule – Deer or Rocky Mountain Blacktail, and The Wapti or Round – Horned Elk.

Of note are two of the last three chapters. In Wilderness Reserves; The Yellowstone Park, the president discusses at length Yellowstone Park and his 1903 visit there with John Burroughs. This chapter condemns professional hunting for markets – the "real offender" in the destruction of game – and urges meaningful hunting laws across the country. Roosevelt also calls for the establishment of large tracks of wilderness. The chapter concludes with an often-quoted passage:

> Surely our people do not understand even
> yet the rich heritage that is theirs. There can
> be nothing in the world more beautiful than

the Yosemite, the groves of giant sequoias and redwoods, the Canyon of the Colorado, the Canyon of the Yellowstone, the Three Tetons; and our people should see that they are preserved for their children and their children's children forever, with their majestic beauty all unmarred.

The final chapter is simply called At Home. It describes the joy Roosevelt took in the wildlife at Sagamore Hill, his home in New York, and Washington, D.C., especially in the songs and habits of the many birds. Roosevelt dedicated the book to John Burroughs: "Every lover of outdoor life must feel a sense of affectionate obligation to you. Your writings appeal to all who care for the life of the woods and the fields. ... It is a good thing for our people that you should have lived; and surely no man can wish to have said more about him."

The president's Fifth Annual Message to Congress was presented on December 5, 1905. Again he stressed the need for reform of public land laws. Under existing laws, he pointed out, great holdings and monopolies continued to be created and to flourish while the purpose of the acts, settlement, languished. Although the perversion of the laws was now, he said, "more generally known, the existing laws did not furnish effective remedies."

Roosevelt commended the progress of reclamation and advocated the extension of the act to Texas. He also observed that providing water was encouraging settlement of the West, offsetting, in part, the problems created by the other public-land laws.

His assessment of forestry was brief. "Since the consolidation of all Government forests in the National Forest Service there has been a rapid and notable gain in the usefulness of the forest reserves to the people and in public appreciation of their value." Although in his previous address he simply acknowledged minor "misunderstanding and complaint," now, flush with victory, he could now observe that all "organized opposition to the forest preserves in the West has disappeared." Further, he asserted, the forest policy of his administration "appears to enjoy the unbroken support of the people" as well as the "great users of timber."

With regard to national parks, he recommended that the national parks in or adjacent to the forest reserves be transferred to the forest service. He further recommended that the forest reserves to the south and east of Yellowstone be incorporated into the park to better protect the winter range of its elk herds.

The President thanked California for the gift of Yosemite and urged Congress to accept it and appropriate necessary money for a Yosemite National Park (In 1864, the federal government gave the Yosemite Valley to California conditioned upon its use as a park. In 1890, the federal government established its own Yosemite National Park surrounding the valley. In 1905, California passed legislation to recede the valley.) He further encouraged New York to protect Niagara Falls or follow the lead of California and donate the falls to the federal government so that it might establish a national park. Again, he asked Congress to establish a Grand Canyon National Park.

Finally, Roosevelt turned his attention to the protection of bison. He noted that the herds were small and their hides still in demand. He urged Congress to create a park like the Wichita reserve for the protection of the remaining herds.

As it had done before, Congress responded to the President's message. On June 11, it accepted the gift of the Yosemite Valley from California. Congress did not give the Grand Canyon national park status but, in November, established the Grand Canyon Game Preserve.

After prior unsuccessful efforts, Congress passed legislation establishing Mesa Verde National Park. In doing so, Congress directed the Secretary of the Interior to preserve "the ruins and other works and relics of prehistoric primitive man" within the park. Roosevelt signed this legislation on May 26, 1906.

Most significantly, Congress passed and the President signed into law the Act for the Preservation of American Antiquities. Principally out of concern for the damage to historic sites, various bills were introduced in Congress from 1900 through 1906.[98] Within a short period, Congress had three similar bills under consideration. In April 1900, a bill requested by the McKinley administration was introduced. It went beyond the preservation of antiquities and was intended as a comprehensive national parks act. It was intended to allow a president to "set aside and reserve tracts of public land, which for their scenic beauty, natural wonders or curiosities, ancient ruins or relics, or other objects of scientific or historic interest, or springs of medicinal or other properties it is desirable to protect and utilize in the interest of the public."[99]

Various bills and legislative efforts ebbed and flowed for the next five years. Finally, in 1906, Congress passed the Act for the Preservation of American Antiquities. President Roosevelt signed it into law on June 8, 1906. The Antiquities Act gave the president authority to declare "National Monuments" – government owned lands identified as "historic landmarks, historic and prehistoric structures, and other objects of historic or scientific interest." Once designated, national monuments were protected against injury and destruction except under permit by the federal government. Presidents were limited, however, to designating the minimum amount of land necessary to achieve the stated purposes of the designation.

Under this new authority, Roosevelt created, on September 24, 1906, Devils Tower National Monument, a tower of igneous rock that rises hundreds of feet above its sandstone base in South Dakota. Following, on December 8, 1906, were: El Moro National Monument, an ancient graffiti site in New Mexico; Montezuma's Castle National Monument, a southwestern cliff dwelling; and the Petrified Forest National Monument containing mineralized remains of Mesozoic forests. In 1906 Roosevelt also designated or reconfigured approximately 50 forest reserves.

On an ominous note, in 1906, crews from several Japanese vessels raided St. Paul Island, Alaska to slaughter fur seals within a protected seal rookery. Americans drove off the Japanese with force of arms. Five of the marauders were killed, two wounded, and twelve captured.

On December 3, 1906, in his Sixth Annual Message, Roosevelt denounced the incident. He also denounced the practice of pelagic sealing (the killing of seals at sea) which usually included the killing of pregnant females resulting in the death of the fetus and the nursing pup born the prior year. "No damage whatever is done to the herd by the carefully regulated killing on land," Roosevelt said. "[T]he custom of pelagic sealing is solely responsible for all of the present evil, and is alike indefensible from the economic standpoint and from the standpoint of humanity." Treaties to control pelagic sealing were ineffective, the President asserted. By way of example, he reported that in 1897, an estimated 400,000 seals were slaughtered at sea; an estimated 300,000 pups starved as a result. Since 1868, when President Grant designated the Pribilof Islands in Alaska as a protected area for fur seals, the herd declined from 4,700,000 animals to less than 200,000.

In discussing the Japanese slaughter of the protected St. Paul Island herd, the President noted that "[n]early all of the seals killed were females and the work was done with frightful barbarity. Many of the seals appear to have been skinned alive and many were found half skinned and still alive." If Congress could not pass adequate legislation and proper international agreements negotiated, the President suggested that it might be more appropriate to humanely slaughter the entire herd in order to stop the barbaric practices of skinning animals alive and leaving pups to die of starvation.

Roosevelt requested legislation making it a crime to enter U.S. waters to kill seals and allowing the forfeiture of vessels involved. He further requested legislation making the possession of seal skins and sealing equipment clear evidence of a violation.

The President announced his prior shipment of vessels, arms, and ammunition to assist in the repelling of any future outrages. He further noted that a U.S. vessel was being dispatched to the sealing grounds the following season.

Roosevelt's Sixth Annual Message on the forest management system and reclamation were muted compared to what he had said in previous years. He noted that efforts by the administration were fruitful and beneficial for the Rocky Mountain and Great Plains states. He also advocated extending the forest reserve program to New England's White Mountains and to the southern Appalachians, each requiring congressional action.

Two weeks after delivering his Sixth Annual Message to Congress, Roosevelt transmitted a special message to Congress about the land laws. He noted his grave concern "at the extremely unsatisfactory condition of the public land laws and at the prevalence of fraud under their present provisions."

The President requested legislation regulating the harvest of timber by the railroads and for the transfer of certain railroad lands into the forest reserve system. He also requested a $5 million appropriation to allow the Forest Service to install the infrastructure necessary for the "proper maintenance of the forest reserves – trails, fences, cabins for the rangers, bridges, telephone lines, and other items of equipment without which the reserves cannot be handled to advantage, cannot be protected properly and cannot contribute as they should to the general welfare." Again, he requested transfer of the national parks to the Department of Agriculture. Finally, he recommended the regulation and closing of the open range to eliminate over grazing and range disputes.

Despite Roosevelt's earlier pronouncements of near universal support of his forest policies, more difficulties lay ahead. In February 1907, Congress passed new legislation forbidding the President from designating national forests in Oregon, Washington, Idaho, Montana, Colorado, and Wyoming.

The patron of the legislation was Senator Fulton of Oregon. In speaking for his bill, Senator Fulton stated:

> The truth is, this bureau [of Forestry] is composed of dreamers and theorists, but beyond and outside the domain of their theories and their dreams is the everyday, busy, bustling, throbbing world of human endeavor, where real men are at work producing substantial results. While these chiefs of the Bureau of Forestry sit within their marble halls and theorize and dream of waters conserved, forests and streams protected and preserved through the ag4es and ages, the lowly pioneer is climbing the mountain side, where he will erect his humble cabin, and within the shadow of the whispering pines and the lofty firs of the western forest engage in the laborious work of

carving out for himself and his loved ones a home and dwelling place. It is of him I think and for him I shall take my stand today.[100]

In actuality, land fraud, as practiced by prominent Oregonians, had thwarted the lonely pioneers from establishing humble cabins on the mountain side. Roosevelt's policies and actions were committed to family homesteading and resource protection.

Two years earlier, Roosevelt had made this clear to Idaho Senator Weldon Brinton Heyburn. The Senator had sent the President various newspaper clipping purporting to show opposition to the President's forest reserve policies. Roosevelt responded:

> With few exceptions, these articles, though the writers do not always seem to know it, are in direct accord with the present policy of the Government in the establishment of National Forest Reserves. The various writers agree that forest reserves in southern Idaho are absolutely essential to the general prosperity of that region. It is admitted that there the forests must be protected and wisely used for the regulation of the waterflow and the benefit of the settlers on vast areas of arid lands soon to be irrigated. This sentiment speaks well for the work of the Forest Service in this region and seems to indicate that the recommendations of its field men are so far heartily approved of, notwithstanding the fact that you yourself have opposed, by written protest, the establishment of each and every one of the new reserves in southern Idaho.

*   *   *

The other clippings you send relate to [Republican] party matters, and strive to make it appear that the forest reserve question in Idaho is a matter of political importance. Now when I can properly pay heed to political interests, I will do so; but I will not for one moment consent to sacrifice the interests of the people as a whole to the real or fancied interests of any individual or political faction. The Government policy in the establishment of National Forest Reserves has been in effect for some time; its good results are already evident; it is a policy emphatically in the interest of the people as a whole; and especially the people of the west; I believe they cordially approve it; and I do not intend to abandon it.

Senator Fulton's legislation passed on February 25; if signed, into law it would be strip Roosevelt's authority to establish national forests in six western states. The restriction was included as part of the appropriation bill for the Department of Agriculture to discourage Roosevelt from vetoing it.

Over the next few days, Gifford Pinchot and his staff worked to identify appropriate forested lands in those six western states for inclusion into the national forest reserve system. Sixteen million acres spread among 32 proposed forest reserves were identified and presented to Roosevelt. Roosevelt designated the proposed reserves on March 1 and 2, 1907. On March 4, he signed Fulton's legislation.

Roosevelt's official memorandum concerning the action was careful and clever. He claimed his action benefited Congress!

The necessary proclamation under existing law now comes before me and the question is presented whether I should refrain from acting under the existing law because there is now under consideration by Congress a proposal to change the law so as to require Congressional action upon the establishing of such forest reserves. If I did not act, reserves which I consider very important for the interests of the United States would be wholly or in part dissipated before Congress has an opportunity again to consider the matter; while under the action which I propose to take they will be preserved; and if Congress differs from me in this opinion it will have full opportunity in the future to take such position as it may desire....

Failure on my part to sign these proclamations would mean that immense tracts of valuable timber would fall into the hands of the lumber syndicates before Congress has an opportunity to act....[101]

However, Roosevelt gloated in private: "The opponents of the Forest Service turned handsprings in their wrath, and dire were the threats against the Executive; but the threats could not be carried out, and were really only a tribute to the efficiency of our action."[102]

Western legislators continued to seethe. In June, Colorado officials convened a Public Lands Convention in Denver. The purpose: to mobilize opposition to the administration's conservation programs on public lands. No direct or immediate results materialized. However, two years later, after Roosevelt left office, an emboldened Congress would deny funding for all presidential commissions unless authorized by it.

During the year, eight additional national forests (a new term created at Pinchot's request by the March 4 legislation, replacing "forest reserves") were created or redefined in area. Also in 1907, Roosevelt established five new bird reservations: Shell Keys National Bird Reservation in Louisiana; Three Arch Rocks National Bird Reservation along the Oregon coast; and Flattery Rocks, Copalis Rocks, and Quillayute Needles National Bird Reserves along the Washington coast.

Five new national monuments also were established by Roosevelt in 1907: Chaco Canyon National Monument in New Mexico (Anasazi buildings from around 850 A.D. through 1125); Cinder Cone and Lassen Peak National Monuments in California; the Gila Cliff Dwelling National Monument in New Mexico; and Tonto National Monument in Arizona (prehistoric cliff dwellings).

In March 1907, President Roosevelt established the Inland Waterways Commission to advise him on transportation and conservation issues. Appointed were Theodore E. Burton, Francis G. Newlands, W.J. McGee, William Warner, John H. Bankhead, Alexander Mackenzie, F.H. Newell, Gifford Pinchot, and Herbert Knox Smith. The commission was to develop a comprehensive plan for waterway transportation throughout the United States. In the course of the commission's deliberations, it determined that an assessment of the nation's resources, including water, would be useful. During a trip down the Mississippi River in May, the Commission also recommended to Roosevelt a national conservation conference with all of the governors. The President agreed.

In announcing the conference, Roosevelt's invitations noted the decline of national resources and their utmost importance to the health of the nation. He wrote, "it seems to me time for the country to take account of its natural resources and to inquire how long they are likely to last."[103] Continuing, Roosevelt reaffirmed that there "is no other question now before the Nation of equal gravity with the question of the conservation of our natural resources; and I add...that it is the plain duty of those of us who, for the moment are responsible, to make inventory of the natural resources which have been handed down to us, to forecast as well as we may the needs of the future, and so to handle the great sources of our prosperity as not to destroy in advance all hope of the prosperity of our descendants."[104]

An editorial in *Century Magazine* in November 1907 complimented Roosevelt on his conservation efforts particularly the transfer of the forest reserves from Interior to Agriculture, the retrocession of Yosemite to the United States, and the attempted establishment of Appalachian forest reserves. Noting the accomplishment of the first two, the editorial expressed hope that the impending Governors Conference would help to bring about the third.

In preparation for publication, the magazine solicited feedback from the invited governors and published responses. The Governor of Virginia, for example, wrote:

I most extremely favor proper legislation for the protection and preservation of our forest reserves. The matter is of such urgent importance that it cannot be further delayed without great detriment to the best interest of the country. It is one of the most important matters that will be discussed in the conference of governors which the President has called to meet this May...I shall attend and shall gladly cooperate in aiding in the passage of such measures and the inauguration of such policies as will tend to the preservation of the natural resources of this nation.

When Roosevelt presented His Seventh Annual Message to Congress in December 1907, he was facing his last full year as President. He again was on the defensive.

Several pages of his address were devoted to a broad defense of the Department of Agriculture. "When the Department of Agriculture was founded," he said, "there was much sneering as to its usefulness. No Department of the Government, however, has more emphatically vindicated its usefulness, and none save the Post-Office Department comes so continually and intimately into touch with the people."

He then went into a discussion of natural resources and, obliquely, the Department of Agriculture.

> The conservation of our natural resources and their proper use constitute the fundamental problem which underlies almost every other problem of our National life. We must entertain for our civilization the adequate material basis without which that civilization can not exist. We must show foresight, we must look ahead....[T]here must be a realization of the fact that to waste, to destroy, our natural resources, to skin and exhaust the land instead of using it so as to increase its usefulness, will result in undermining in the days of our children the very prosperity which we ought by right hand down to them amplified and developed.

President Roosevelt called for massive engineering on the nation's rivers, particularly the Mississippi and the Columbia. He envisioned a system of locks and dams to provide internal highways of commerce, flood control, hydroelectric power, and water storage.

Again, he called for amendment of the public land laws. He reminded Congress of the findings of the Public Lands Commission three years earlier – that there was great fraud and consolidation of public lands in the hands of a few. He further decried the "enormous waste caused by unrestricted grazing upon the open range." He again asked

59

Congress to act upon the commission's recommendations. Included among them was that the government fence and lease lands under management programs designed to reduce waste. Further, he recommended, property should be conveyed only to small ranchers or farmers upon assurances that they would keep it.

Roosevelt continued by addressing waste:

> Optimism is a good characteristic, but if carried to an excess it becomes foolishness. We are prone to speak of the resources of this country as inexhaustible; this is not so. The mineral wealth of the country, the coal, iron, oil, gas, and the like, does not reproduce itself, and therefore is certain to be exhausted ultimately; and wastefulness in dealing with it-today means that our descendents will feel the exhaustion a generation or two before they otherwise would. But there are certain other forms of waste which could be entirely stopped – the waste of soil by washing, for instances, which is among the most dangerous of all wastes now in progress in the United States, is easily preventable so that this present enormous loss of fertility is entirely unnecessary. The preservation or replacement of the forest is one of the most important means of preventing the loss.

He warned about the depletion of forests. Trees were being harvested three times faster than they were being replenished. Twenty percent of the nation's forests were now in the national forests. Loss of the forests could be controlled, however, by an active Congress - not only through expansion of national forests and reform of the land laws, but also through extension of national forests in the East.

Finally, he warned about the impending destruction of the Alaskan salmon fishery. "Gradually, by reason of lack of proper laws, this industry is being ruined; it should now be taken in charge, and effectively protected, by the United States Government."

The year 1908 was busy and productive for the President and conservation. It began with the designation of Muir Woods National Monument. In 1903, when the President was with John Muir, Muir reportedly pushed Roosevelt to use his influence preserving the magnificent redwood and sequoia trees. Roosevelt got his opportunity in 1908. Congressman and Mrs. William Kent gave the federal government the 295 acres of old growth redwoods; some were 250 feet in height and 12 feet in diameter. Roosevelt promptly designated it Muir Woods National Monument. Roosevelt subsequently acknowledged Muir as a great factor in preserving the "wonderful canyons, giant trees, slopes of flower-spangled hillsides – which make California a veritable Garden of the Lord."

On January 11, 1908, Roosevelt designated an astonishing 800,000 acres of the Grand Canyon a national monument; under the terms of the Antiquities Act, this was the "smallest area compatible with proper care and management of the objects to be protected."

January 16 saw the designation of the Pinnacles National Monument in central California near the Salinas Valley. The monument takes its name from towering rock spires. When designated, Pinnacles was 2,060 acres; its boundaries have been increased five times by presidents and once by Congress to its present size - 24,500 acres. Roosevelt also created Jewel Cave National Monument in February and Natural Bridges National Monument in April, and the Lewis and Clark Cavern National Monument in May.

May 13 through 15, 1908, Roosevelt hosted the Conference of Governors. The list of attendees was nothing short of spectacular – the President and Vice President, seven cabinet members, the entire Supreme Court, 34 state governors, representatives from the other 12 states, and the governors from all of the territories, including Alaska, Hawaii, and Puerto Rico, members of Congress, four special guests, representatives of sixty eight national societies, and various other guests.

Roosevelt delivered the keynote address, stressing familiar themes: forest conservation, exhaustion of resources, reclamation, and protection of resources. For the next three days, committees met and papers were presented, and a draft report of the conference was prepared. Roosevelt used the final report of the conference during the waning days of his administration, to push for necessary action by Congress. The conference report recommended continued efforts to protect timber supplies and water quality and quantity. It further advocated a strengthening of the administration's conservation policies as well as future conferences to foster cooperation among the states and the federal government.[105]

Looking back on the conference several months later, Roosevelt announced that it "confirmed and strengthened in the minds of our people the conviction that our natural resources are being consumed, wasted, and destroyed at a rate which threatens them with exhaustion."[106]

Another recommendation of the conference was that the each state create a commission on the conservation of resources to cooperate with the federal government. A majority of the states did so. The President reciprocated and appointed a federal Commission on the Conservation of Natural Resources to advise him and facilitate cooperation with the states. The Commission on the Conservation of Natural Resources was divided into three working groups, waters, forests, and lands and minerals. Gifford Pinchot was named chairman of the executive committee.

In establishing the commission, Roosevelt observed that "[t]he Commission must keep in mind the further fact that all natural resources are so related that their use may be, and should be, co-ordinated." [107] Roosevelt asked the Congress for $ 25,000 to support the work of the commission and was refused. Accordingly, he issued an executive order directing all agencies to cooperate with its work. Anticipating the end of his term, the President directed the commission to present at least a preliminary report by January 1, 1909.

Also in May 1908, the National Bison Range was created by Congress on land purchased by the Roosevelt administration for this purpose. Although it was the fourth game preserve established during the Roosevelt administration, this was the first time that land was purchased for wildlife protection. The National Bison Range is now home to over 450 bison. The 18,500-acre range also is home to elk, deer, bear, coyote, and more than 200 species of birds.

By June, the Inland Waterways Commission delivered its preliminary report. The President found it "excellent in every way." It outlined a general plan of waterway improvement, which, if adopted, would yield increased benefits to the American people. Pending action by Congress, Roosevelt directed the commission to continue its work and he issued an executive order directing all federal agencies to give the commission access to their records.

July 1908 saw a massive overhauling of the national forests. Approximately 125 national forests were created or reconfigured. Several more were established later that year.

Roosevelt also designated two other monuments in 1908 – Tumacacori and Wheeler. Tumacacori National Monument in Arizona protected a church built in 1822. Wheeler National Monument in Colorado was designated to protect "volcanic formations ...of unusual scientific interest as illustrating erratic erosion." [108]

Roosevelt also designated a number of bird reservations. Of those still in existence or otherwise under federal protection are the Tortugas National Bird Reservation in Florida, the Key West National Bird Reservation, Klamath Lake National Wildlife Refuge in Oregon, Lake Malheur National Bird Reservation in Oregon, and Pine Island, Matlachha Pass, and Island Bay on Florida's west coast.

Klamath Lake was the first bird reservation established within the boundaries of a reclamation project. Because Congress was not appropriating money for the bird reserves, perhaps the President believed he could bootstrap reclamation funds for wildlife preservation. In any event, there was conflicting purposes between a wildlife refuge, established for preservation, and a reclamation project, designed to foster development. The conflict apparently took its toll; Roosevelt designated 19 bird reserves which are no longer in existence. Most of these are the reclamation overlay refuges, including seventeen established on February 25, 1909.

On December 8, Roosevelt presented Congress his eighth and final annual message. He began the environmental portion with a common refrain: "If there is any one duty which more than any we owe it to our children and to our children's children to perform at once, it is to save the forests of this country, for they constitute the first and most important element in the natural resources of the country."

Roosevelt warned of the damage to the soil and rivers already evident in some parts of the country. To drive home the point, he provided a detailed report prepared by the Department of Agriculture on conditions in China. A foreshadowing of the dust bowl of the thirties, the President observed that the lesson of deforestation in China is a lesson which mankind should have learned many times. Denudation leaves naked soil; then gullying cuts down to the bare rock; and rock-waste buries the bottom-lands. "When the soil is gone, men must go; and the process does not take long."

On rivers, Roosevelt reported waste and inefficiency in efforts to improve navigation. He advocated a single permanent commission authorized to coordinate the work of all government departments relating to waterways.

As to parks, he recommended management reorganization for those parks adjacent to national forests. The parks were managed by the Department of Interior; the Army policed the parks and provided road construction. Roosevelt advocated a superintendent for each park assisted by a professional staff of "scouts or rangers." He further recommended that Yellowstone and Yosemite be kept as national playgrounds; "in both, all wild things should be protected and the scenery kept wholly unmarred."

He concluded with a well-deserved pat on his own shoulder: "I am happy to say that I have been able to set aside in various parts of the country small, well-chosen tracts of ground to serve as sanctuaries and nurseries for wild creatures."

The year was finished with the Joint Conservation Conference, also known as the Second governor's Conference held on December 8. The Joint Conservation Conference was convened to accept the final report issued by the Conference of Governors and keep the conservation momentum going. Thirty one governors or their representatives attended. Twenty six new conservation commissions from various states also attended. The Joint Conservation Conference voiced strong support for the work of the President's National Conservation Commission and encouraged it to continue its good work.

A month later, Roosevelt sent Congress the report prepared by the first Conference of Governors. According to Roosevelt, the report was "irrefutable proof that the conservation of our resources is the fundamental question before this nation, and that our first and greatest task is to set our house in order and begin to live within our means." The summary of the report provided by the President in his transmittal reaffirmed his major themes on water, forests, and public lands.

In the remaining two months of his term, Roosevelt set aside five additional national forests, 26 bird reservations, and one national monument, Mount Olympus National Monument. Mount Olympus, designated on March 2, 1909, just two days before Roosevelt left office, covered 600,000 acres within the 2 million acre Olympic National Forest. The stated reasons for the designation were the scientific interest in the glaciers and the Olympic Elk, also known as Roosevelt Elk. In 1937, President Franklin D. Roosevelt helped secure national park status for the monument and expand its boundaries. In 1988, 95 percent of the park was designated "wilderness" thereby securing added protection against encroachment. Today, Olympic National Park contains three distinct environments: glacier-capped mountains; old growth temperate rain forest; and coastal beaches. Within the park are the summer range and breeding grounds of the Roosevelt elk and other "well-chosen tracts of ground to serve as sanctuaries and nurseries for wild creatures."

On March 4, 1909, Roosevelt's presidency ended.

NATIONAL FORESTS

From the beginning of the "forest reserve" system through the end of the Roosevelt presidency, forest policy was controversial. Roosevelt struggled to hold onto gains and to build on them.

Throughout the end of the 19th century and beginning of the 20th, U.S policy favored liquidation of land and resources to promote settlement; Westerners believed it was their right to use federal land and resources (timber, water, stone, and minerals) as necessary. To many, depletion and ruination of the federal forests was evident. As early as 1877, the Secretary of the Interior warned about the alarming status of the nations forests:

> The rapidity with which this country is being stripped of its forests must alarm every thinking man. It has been estimated by good authority that, if we go on at the present rate, the supply of timber in the United States will, in less than twenty years, fall considerably short of our home necessities. How disastrously the destruction of the forests of a country affects the regularity of the water supply in its rivers necessary for navigation, increases the frequency of freshets and inundation, dries up springs, and transforms fertile agricultural districts into barren wastes, is a matter of universal experience the world over. It is the highest time that we should turn our attention to this subject, which so seriously concerns our national prosperity.[109]

Or, as naturalist John Muir succinctly put it 14 years later, "our forests...have been mismanaged long and come desperately near being like smashed eggs and spilt milk." [110]

In 1891, Congress passed a comprehensive forest act, which, in part, authorized the President to set aside and reserve public lands: "[T]he President of the United States may, from time to time, set apart and reserve...public lands...as public reserves."[111] The purpose of forest reserves was not specified. However, the effect of the act was to curtail some of the other laws which permitted the public to acquire the land or harvest the resources. Closing of the public domain, even a part of it, was unthinkable (if not un-American) to many. However, by the second Cleveland administration, the prevailing understanding was that reserves were, in fact, reserved from development. As Muir noted in writing about the creation of forest reserves, "[t]here will be a period of indifference on the part of the rich, sleepy with wealth, and of the toiling millions, sleepy with poverty, most of whom never saw a forest; a period of screaming protest and objection from the plunderers who are as unconscionable and enterprising as Satan. But light is surely coming, and the friends of destruction will preach and bewail in vain." [112]

Subsequent administrative actions, Congressional hearings, and draft legislation focused on a consensus – the forest reserves were designed to manage logging and to protect watersheds.[113] Indeed, one historian of the national forest system has suggested that "it would have been more accurate to label the reserves 'water reserves,' but forests were the most visible component, so forest reserves they became."[114]

In 1891, approximately 2.5 million acres were placed into reserves. Another 3 million acres were designated the following year. In 1893, an additional 12 million acres were set aside, including the 4.5-million acre Cascade Forest

Reserve. With these designations, protests grew. In particular, the Oregon congressional delegation worked, unsuccessfully, to reverse the Cascade Forest Reserve. Amid the protests and lack of serious management or legislative review, designation of forest reserves became moribund.

Early in 1896, Secretary of the Interior assembled a commission to study issues concerning the forest reserves. The Forestry Commission looked at the issue of ownership of the federal forests and management of the forest reserves and recommended legislation necessary to secure proper management. Based upon the work of the Forest Commission, the Secretary of the Interior recommended to President Grover Cleveland, on February 6, 1897, that the forest reserves be increased. Cleveland accepted the recommendations and on February 22, 1897 established 13 forest reserves encompassing more than 21 million acres.

Designation of 21 million acres caused howls of protest in the West. Cleveland vetoed repeal legislation on his last day in office. Because the repeal was in the appropriations bill, Cleveland left his successor, President McKinley, with no money for operations. A special session of Congress was called, funds were appropriated, and a compromise on the February 22 designations was made; the compromise permitted the plundering of the 21 million acres for nine months before the designations became effective.

The legislative compromise also remedied the silence about the purpose of the forest reserves. Congress stated that the purpose of forest reserves is "to improve and protect the forest within the reservation, or for securing favorable conditions of water flows, and to furnish a continuous supply of timber for the use and necessities of citizens of the United States...." Further, timbering and mineral extractions were made subject to federal regulation. This act, known as the

Organic Act of 1897, set in place for the next 50 years the basic management policies for national forests.

The law also provided for management of the forest reserves by the Secretary of the Interior who was given management responsibility and charged with the appointment of rangers. This was handled through the Department of the Interior's General Land Office. In practice, appointments were in close consultation with senators from affected states and, because the spoil system was still a component in American politics, appointments became political.

Additional forests were added during McKinley's first term and the total protected acreage rose to almost 47 million acres. However, the acreage began to slip and when Theodore Roosevelt became President, forest reserves encompassed 46,328,000 million acres and waste and fraud continued to ravage the federal holdings. As John Muir noted, "a change from robbery and ruin to a permanent rational policy is urgently needed."[115]

President Roosevelt, assisted by Gifford Pinchot, provided the needed "rational policy." From the start, Roosevelt recognized the importance of forests. As he told Congress in his first annual message:

> Public opinion throughout the United States has moved steadily toward a just appreciation of the value of the forests, whether planted or of natural growth. The great part played by them in the creation and maintenance of the national wealth is now mournfully realized than ever before. Wise forest protection does not mean the withdrawal of forest resources, whether wood, water, or grass from contributing their full share to the welfare of the people, but on the

contrary gives the assurance of larger and more certain supplies. The fundamental idea of forestry is the protection of forests by use. Forest protection is not an end of itself, it is a means to increase and sustain the resources of our country and the industries which depend upon them.

Roosevelt identified conservation of the nation's resources as the fundamental problem facing the Country and addressed it often.

By the time Roosevelt left office, millions of acres would be added, more than three times the acreage existing when he became President. The only major additions to the national forest system after Roosevelt's presidency were the eastern forests, something Roosevelt advocated but could not accomplish without congressional approval.

Roosevelt's success was made possible by the able assistance of his chief forester, Gifford Pinchot. Gifford Pinchot graduated from Yale in 1889 and then traveled to France and Germany to study forestry. There, his core belief was formed - forestry essentially is the farming of trees. This belief eventually matured into his detailed beliefs on conservation.

After Pinchot returned to the United States, he earned his living by managing the forest at the Vanderbilt's North Carolina estate, Biltmore. By 1898, he became head of the U.S. Department of Agriculture's Forestry Division under President McKinley, a position he would hold for 13 years under three presidents, McKinley, Roosevelt, and Taft. As the head of U.S. forestry, he would have extraordinary impact on forest management particularly after full authority for forest management was transferred to his department in 1905.

As discussed elsewhere in this book, Pinchot was a strong advocate of wise use. So committed was he that he further believed that all forests should be cut to eliminate their wildness so that the second growth could be properly "managed":

> Full utilization of the productive power of the Forests...does not take place until after the land has been cut over in accordance with the rules of scientific forestry. The transformation from a wild to a cultivated forest must be brought about by the ax. Hence, the importance of substituting as fast as practicable, the actual use for the mere hoarding of timber.[116]

The establishment and proper management of national forests were controversial. But, by the time Roosevelt left office in March 1909, he had designated approximately 148 million acres of national forest in twenty different states.[117] Many of these designations have been consolidated into larger national forests. The national forests designated by Present Roosevelt are listed below their current names and organized by state.

ALASKA

Chugach National Forest – Chugach is an amazing 5.6-million-acre forest along the south central coast of Alaska. Prince William Sound and the Kenai Peninsula are within Chugach. Chugach offers a variety of activities, including wildlife watching, hiking, camping, fishing, and kayaking. Chugach was established on July 23, 1907. Roosevelt added additional land the following year.

Tongass National Forest – Tongass embraces 17 million acres along the Alaska panhandle. President Roosevelt created it on September 10, 1907. The Alexander

Archipelago National Forest, also established by Roosevelt, was added to Tongass in July 1908. Coastal rainforests and numerous islands shrouded with western hemlocks and Sitka spruce characterize Tongass. Visits to Tongass' glaciers and fjords are magical. The wildlife watching and fishing opportunities are abundant.

ARIZONA

Apache-Sitgreaves National Forest - The Apache and the Sitgreaves National Forests were each established on July 1, 1908. Subsequently, they were consolidated and are now known as Apache-Sitgreaves National Forest. It is located in Arizona's central highlands, including the White Mountains. Douglas fir and Ponderosa pine dominate forested areas. Apache-Sitgreaves offers a rich mixture of uses including winter ski and snowmobile venues. It has deer, pronghorn, elk, mountain lions, bear, and wolves. The Blue Range Primitive Area is a particularly spectacular part of Apache-Sitgreaves.

Coronado National Forest – Coronado stretches from the southern lowland deserts to the Rocky Mountains. Coronado contains a hidden jewel for the bird watching enthusiast – Bird Cave Creek Canyon. This oasis surrounded by desert attracts migrating birds along the flyway. Coronado was created on July 1, 1908 through the consolidation of three other forests established by President Theodore Roosevelt. Over the years, four other Roosevelt-designated forests were consolidated with Coronado.

Prescott National Forest – On December 30, 1907, Roosevelt created the Verde National Forest. On July1, 1908, he combined it with Prescott. Prescott runs from the Sonora Desert to the Bradshaw Mountains. With over 450 miles of trails, it is an outdoor enthusiasts delight. Of particular interest is Sycamore Canyon, also known as the "Little Grand Canyon."

Tonto National Forest - Tonto is a 3-million-acre blend of desert, mountains, and canyons in central Arizona. Roosevelt established it on October 3, 1905. Twice, in 1908, Roosevelt added land. Among its features is the Apache Trail National Forest Scenic Byway. Visitors may take a raft trip down the Verde River.

ARKANSAS

Ouachita National Forest - President Roosevelt established the 1-million-acre Arkansas National Forest on December 18, 1907. In 1926, the name was changed to Ouachita. Ouachita is dominated by the sharp-ridged Ouachita Mountains covered by a mix of hardwoods and pine. Visitors may float down the Ouachita River or hike along the Ouachita Trail.

Ozark – St. Francis National Forest – This 1-million-acre forest is in the Ozark Mountains in northeastern Arkansas. President Roosevelt established the Ozark National Forest on March 6, 1908. In 1963, it was combined with the St. Francis National Forest. The Ozark Highlands Trail winds for 165 miles through the forest.

CALIFORNIA

Cleveland National Forest – The Cleveland National forest in southern California is in three major sections. It is convenient to both Los Angeles and San Diego. The forest embraces the San Mateo Mountains. This hot, dry forest is dominated by chaparral with Coulter pine in the mountains. Four wilderness sections are designated in Cleveland. President Roosevelt established Cleveland on July 1, 1908

Eldorado National Forest – Eldorado lies within and to the west of northern California's Sierra Nevada Mountains. Dominated by chaparral, conifer, and pine, the forest features 10,000-foot granite peaks and sheer-walled canyons. Three wilderness areas are contained within Eldorado – Desolation, Mokelumne, and Caples Creek.

Inyo National Forest – Inyo is an impressive 2-million-acre national forest stretching for 165 miles along the California-Nevada border. Located in Inyo is the 14,496-foot Mount Whitney, the highest mountain in the lower 48. Also in Inyo is Mono Lake which receives water from various streams but has no outlet. Over the yeas this has caused the lake to form a saline habitat whose brine shrimp feed thousands of migrating birds.

Klamath National Forest – The Klamath National Forest straddles the California and Oregon line and is dominated by Mount Shasta. President Roosevelt established Klamath on May 6, 1905. The diverse habitat, with its high desert, mountains, rain forest, streams, and 89 lakes, allows for a wide range of wildlife and plants including more than 270 species of birds. Rafting and kayaking the Salmon and Klamath Rivers are some of the many mixed uses available.

Lassen National Forest - Lassen Peak National Forest was established on June 2, 1905. President Roosevelt changed the name to Lassen and adjusted the boundaries on July 1, 1908. Lassen is in northern California and surrounds the Lassen National Volcanic Park. Although the southern Cascades are the dominant feature, Lassen embraces part of the Sierra Nevada Mountains, Modoc Plateau, and Great Basin. Of particular interest is the 85-mile Lassen Scenic Byway forming a loop through the forest.

Los Padres National Forest – President Roosevelt established the Monterey National Forest on June 25, 1906 and Pinnacles National Forest on July 18, 1906. They were consolidated into what is now known as Los Padres National Forest in the central California coastal mountains, stretching 220 miles from Big Sur for 220 miles to Santa Barbara.

More than 1,200 miles of trails provide for rugged hiking and breath-taking vistas.

Modoc National Forest – Established in 1904 and expanded in 1908, Modoc is a 2- million-acre forest displaying California's volcanic history. Modoc has diverse habitats, including high desert, lava caves, pine forests, rugged mountains, hot springs, canyons, meadows, rivers, lakes, and wetlands.

Plumas National Forest – Plumas National Forest contains 1 million acres in northern California. Established March 25, 1905, Plumas' hundreds of miles of trails crisscross streams and rivers making Plumas a thoroughly enjoyable destination. Among Plumas' popular destinations is the 640-foot Feather Falls.

Sequoia National Forest – Sequoia National Forest contains approximately half of the largest living things on earth: sequoias. Three dozen groves of these massive trees are found in Sequoia National Forest. The Trail of a Hundred Giants in the Long Meadow Grove showcases these magnificent trees. President Roosevelt established Sequoia National Forest on July 1, 1908.

Shasta-Trinity National Forest – Trinity National Forest was established on April 29, 1905. Shasta National Forest was established shortly thereafter on October 3, 1905. These forests have been consolidated as Shasta-Trinity. Shasta-Trinity National Forest is in the foothills and mountains of northern California. Among its many peaks is Mount Shasta, a 14,000-foot active volcano. Shasta-Trinity is endowed with five rugged wilderness areas that protect hundreds of thousands of acres.

Tahoe National Forest – President Roosevelt reconfigured Lake Tahoe National Forest on October 3, 1905, and renamed it Tahoe. Additional land was added on September

17, 1906. Tahoe National Forest is north and east of Lake Tahoe in the Sierra Nevada Mountains and surrounding foothills.

COLORADO

Gunnison National Forest – After the 1900 election, Vice President-elect Theodore Roosevelt returned to the western slopes of the Colorado Rockies to hunt. Roosevelt recalled that trip in *Outdoor Pastimes of an American Hunter*: "The midwinter mountain landscape was very beautiful, whether under the brilliant blue sky of the day, or the star light or the glorious moonlight of the night, or when under the dying sun the snowy peaks and the light clouds above, kindled into flame, and sank again to gold and amber and somber purple." On May 2, 1905, Gunnison was established.

Gunnison rises from the depths of the Black Canyon to the 14,000-foot heights of Colorado's western Rockies. Black Canyon, now a national park, is unique with its narrow width, sheer walls, and incredible depths. Gunnison has miles of trails, including 130 miles of the Continental Divide National Scenic Trail.

San Isabel National Forest – In 1900, vice-presidential candidate Theodore Roosevelt concentrated his campaign efforts in the West. During campaign stops in Colorado, he would break from routine and ride through Colorado's vast grandeur.

San Isabel is remarkable for its number of 14,000-foot peaks, 19 in all. These may be enjoyed by use of 800 miles of trails within the 1-million-acre forest. San Isabel receives extra protection through designation of six wilderness areas. San Isabel contains the former Wet Mountain National Forest and the Las Animas National Forest, each established by President Roosevelt.

Uncompahgre National Forest – The Uncompahgre Plateau averages 10,000 feet above sea level. Within this plateau are 100 peaks rising above 13,000 feet and several more reaching 14,000. Rushing water carves deep canyons and gorges. Alpine lakes and dense forests of spruce are features. As Roosevelt wrote: "After the snow-storms, the trees, almost hidden beneath the light feathery masses gave a new and strange look to the mountains, as if they were giant masses of frosted silver. Even the storms had a beauty of their own." Theodore Roosevelt (describing western Rockies of Colorado).

President Roosevelt established the Uncompahgre on June 14, 1905. Over the years, the following forests established by Roosevelt have been consolidated with Uncompahgre – Ouray, Park Range, and San Juan.

FLORIDA

Ocala National Forest – Ocala, north of Orlando, is a lush blend of slow-moving rivers and wetlands hosting palms, live oaks, cypress, other southern hard woods, and dry sand pine scrub. Of particular interest is Alexander Springs, spewing forth 80 million gallons of water per day. Ocala National Forest is a consolidation of two forests designated by Roosevelt, the Ocala and the Choctawhatchee.

IDAHO

Caribou National Forest – Southeast Idaho is home to the 1-million-acre Caribou National Forest. It originally was designated the Pocatello Forest Reserve by President Roosevelt to protect the local watershed. A second Roosevelt designation, the Port Neuf National Forest, was added.

Clearwater National Forest – Clearwater contains 1.8 million acres embracing part of the Bitterroot Mountains. Roosevelt established the forest on July 1, 1908, through consolidation of parts of other forests.

Idaho Panhandle National Forest – Idaho Panhandle National Forest is staggeringly beautiful. It embraces the Bitterroot, Selkirk, Cabinet, and Coeur d'Alene mountains. President Roosevelt described an 1886 trip to the Coeur d' Alenes:

> In a day or so we were in the heart of the vast wooded wilderness. A broad, lonely river ran through its midst, cleaving asunder the mountain chains. Range after range, peak upon peak, the mountains towered on every side, the lower timbered to the top, the higher with bare crests of gray crags, or else hooded with fields of shining snow. The deep valleys lay half in darkness, hemmed in by steep, timbered slopes and straight rock walls.

Salmon-Challis National Forest - This stunning 4.3-million-acre forest is defined by pine-shrouded mountains and the Salmon River that cuts deep canyons along its path. Salmon-Chalis also hosts the largest wilderness area in the lower 48. Wildlife abounds.

Sawtooth National Forest – The Sawtooth, dating to May 29, 1905, contains 2.1 million acres of rugged forest in Idaho and Utah. With more than 1,000 lakes and 3,000 miles of streams and rivers, it is pure delight to the outdoor enthusiast.

Targhee National Forest – Targhee National Forest was established July 1, 1908. It was a consolidation of a portion of the Yellowstone and all of Henrys Lake (established by Roosevelt May 23, 1905). Idaho and Wyoming are host to the 1.8-million-acre Targhee National Forest. The Targhee stretches from desert to 10,000-foot Rocky Mountain peaks.

It includes the Jedediah Smith Wilderness and the Winegar Hole Wilderness areas

MICHIGAN

Ottawa National Forest – Toward the end of his tenure, President Roosevelt established two national forests in Michigan, the Michigan National Forest and the Marquette National Forest. Both are now consolidated as part of the 1-million-acre Ottawa National Forest on Michigan's upper peninsula. Because of the heavy snowfall, Ottawa is a particular favorite of winter sports enthusiasts. Of particular splendor is Sturgeon River Falls within the Sturgeon River Gorge Wilderness.

MINNESOTA

Superior National Forest – Sixty miles north of Duluth, in the northeast corner of Minnesota, lies Superior National Forest. The forest contains 3 million acres with hundreds of lakes dotting its landscape. With so many lakes, Superior is home to the 1-million-acre Boundary Waters Canoe Area Wilderness and its 1,500 miles of canoe trails and 2,000 campsites. President Roosevelt established this national forest in the waning days of his administration, February 13, 1909.

MONTANA

Bitterroot National Forest – On July 1, 1908, Hell Gate National Forest (established October 3, 1905) and Big Hole National Forest (established May 11, 1906) were consolidated with the Bitter Root National Forest and the name was changed to Bitterroot National Forest. This 1.6-million-acre national forest in west central Montana along the Idaho line ties together the Bitterroot and Sapphire Mountains and the Bitterroot River Valley.

Flathead National Forest – One of President Roosevelt's earliest designations (June 9, 1903), the Flathead National Forest abuts the southern and western boundaries of Glacier National Park. The 2.3-million-acre forest encompasses the Scapegoat, Bob Marshall, Great Bear, and Mission Mountain wilderness areas. In addition to majestic scenery, the Flathead is known for its fishing, including fishing for the native west slope cutthroat trout.

Kootenai National Forest – Kootenai is in Montana's northwest corner, abutting northern Idaho and British Columbia. The 2.2-million-acre forest contains the Whitefish, Bitterroot, Purcell, Salish, and Cabinet Mountains. Below the craggy mountains, the Kootenai and Clark Fork rivers define the forest floor. President Roosevelt established Kootenai on August 13, 1906.

Helena National Forest – The 1-million-acre Helena National Forest is located around Helena, Montana. Through this stunning country passes the Continental Divide National ScenicTrail and the Blackfoot and Missouri Rivers. For those less hardy souls, the Helena National Forest provides numerous opportunities for auto touring.

Lolo National Forest – The Lolo is spectacular mountain country. This 2.1-million-acre forest envelops Missoula, Montana, on the western fringe of the state. It was established on September 20, 1906.

Gallatin National Forest – In 1905, President Roosevelt established the Big Belt National Forest. Part of Big Belt was added to Gallatin in 1908. Located in south central Montana, the 2.1-million-acre Gallatin borders the northwest corner of Wyoming and Yellowstone National Park. Gallatin has thousands of miles of trails for summer and winter recreational activities. The Gallatin National Forest protects the headwaters of the Yellowstone, Madison, and Gallatin rivers.

Lewis & Clark National Forest – Lewis & Clark contains all or portions of five forests established by President Roosevelt: Hell Gate, High Mountains, Little Belt Mountains, Little Rockies, and Missoula National Forests. The 1.8-million-acre Lewis & Clark National Forest stretches from the prairie to the Continental Divide.

Custer National Forest – Custer National Forest embraces the Dakota grasslands and the Beartooth Mountains. The Beartooth Scenic Byway provides a breathtaking tour of this incredible country. This forest contains all or part of five national forests established by President Roosevelt: Ekalaka, Long Pine, Otter Forest, Pryor Mountain, and Sioux National Forests. It also has two South Dakota forests established by Roosevelt: Cave Hills and Slim Butte.

NEVADA

Humbolt - Toiyabe National Forest – It is difficult to describe Nevada's Humbolt-Toiyabe National Forest. The Humbolt - Toiyabe National Forest contains 6.1 million acres spread across the length and breadth of Nevada in 10 separate sections. The scope of the forest is as broad and beautiful as Nevada, encompassing mountains, canyons, and deserts. President Roosevelt established 11national forests in Nevada: Charleston (November 5, 1906), Humbolt (July 2, 1908), Independence (November 5, 1906), Tahoe (boundary adjusted October 3, 1905), Moapa (January 21, 1909), Monitor (April 15, 1907), Nevada (February 8, 1909), Ruby Mountains (May 3, 1906), Toiyabe (March 1, 1907), Toquimq (April 15, 1907), and Vegas (February 12, 1907). All are now part of the Humbolt-Toiyabe National Forest.

NEBRASKA

Nebraska National Forest – Early in his presidency, Theodore Roosevelt established two experimental national forests in Nebraska: Dismal River and Niobrara . In 1908, he established a third, the North Platte. All three were consolidated on July 1, 1908, into the Nebraska National Forest. The Dismal River National Forest, now known as the Charles E. Bessey Nursery, continues to provide seedlings to the U.S. Forest Service, Bureau of Land Management, and the Bureau of Indian Affairs in Nebraska, Colorado, South Dakota, Kansas, and Wyoming.

NEW MEXICO

Lincoln National Forest – The Lincoln National Forest runs in a north-south direction through south central New Mexico. It contains three major mountain ranges: the Sacramento, Guadalupe, and Captain. As is common in the New Mexican forests, it stretches from desert to mountains. Lincoln was established on July 26, 1902. In 1905, the Gallinas National Forest was added.

Gila National Forest – In 1905, President Roosevelt changed the name of the Gila River National Forest to Gila. On June 18, 1908, Big Burros National Forest and other lands were added. The Gila is a 3.3-million-acre remote forest stretching from the New Mexican Sonora and Chihuahua deserts to the Rocky Mountains. The Gila is extremely remote and contains the first wilderness area designated. Hundreds of miles of trails enable hikers to discover ancient Mogollon cliff dwellings.

Carson National Forest – President Roosevelt established the Jenez and Taos National Forests on October12, 1905 and November 7, 1906 respectively. On July 1, 1908, Carson was formed from all of Taos and a part of Jemez. Carson National Forest is 1.5 million acres of beauty and joy. Cool summer temperatures and the 300 plus miles of trails lure visitors to enjoy all manner of outdoor recreation.

Santa Fe National Forest – Santa Fe is a 1.6-million-acre national forest formed, in part, from the Jemez National

Forest established by President Roosevelt. The Sangre de Cristo Range, with its 13,000-foot peaks, dominates the eastern portion. Also within the Santa Fe is the Jemez Mountain Range, an active volcano area.

Cibola National Forest – Cibola is a 1.6-million-acre national forest and grassland principally located in New Mexico; it dips into Oklahoma and Texas. Cibola is a land of mountains and wilderness areas and contains all or part of seven Roosevelt-established forests: Datil, Gallinas, Magdalena, Manzano, Mount Taylor, San Mateo, and Zuni.

OREGON

Deschutes National Forest – The 1.85-million-acre Deschutes National Forest along the eastern Cascades is one of the most popular recreational destinations in Oregon, drawing millions of visits each year. It was established on July 1, 1908 from parts of the Blue Mountains, Cascade, and Fremont National Forests. A noteworthy challenge within Deschutes is rafting the Deschutes River with its class IV and V rapids.

Siskiyou National Forest – The Siskiyou National Forest was established on October 5, 1906. On July 1, 1908, Roosevelt added the Coquille National Forest and other lands. Siskiyou contains 1.16 million acres in southwestern Oregon. The Cascades and Coastal Range dominate the forest. Within the forest, the mountains are subject to arctic and tropical weather patterns making for diverse plant species.

Umatilla National Forest – The Umatilla was established on July 1, 1908 from the Heppner National Forest and part of the Blue Mountains National Forest. Umatilla is a 1.4-million-acre forest in the Blue Mountains of northeast Oregon. Most of the forest is valleys separated by ridges and plateaus.

Freemont National Forest - This 1.2-million-acre forest in south central Oregon was established by Roosevelt on September 17, 1906, and expanded on July 1, 1908. High, open land offers good views of the Cascades to the west.

Malheur National Forest – Malheur was created from a portion of Blue Mountains National Forest on July 1, 1908. The 1.7-million-acre forest in the Blue Mountains of eastern Oregon is a blend of high desert and alpine.

Ochoco National Forest – Ochoco was formed from portions of the Roosevelt-established Malheur and Deschutes National Forests. The eastern slopes of the Cascade Mountains in central Oregon are the home of the Ochoco National Forest. In addition to being an important supplier of timber, Ochoco attracts millions of recreational visitors who hike, fish, camp, hunt, and rock climb.

Umpqua National Forest – The Umpqua is largely an old-growth forest with Douglas fir and ponderosa pine. President Roosevelt established the forest on March 2, 1907. The Rogue-Umpqua Scenic Byway offers a grand tour, passing volcanoes, waterfalls, and old-growth forest.

Wallowa-Whitman National Forest – Wallowa-Whitman was established on May 6, 1905. President Roosevelt added additional land in 1907 and 1908. In 1954 it was consolidated with Whitman National Forest and its present name was established. In this 2.3-million-acre forest, the Wallowa Mountains, Blue Mountains, and canyons of the Snake River are distinctive features

Siuslaw National Forest – This forest stretches from the Coastal Mountains to the Pacific Coast dunes. Located within the forest is the Oregon Dunes National Recreation Area. President Roosevelt established Siuslaw on July 1, 1908 from parts of Tillamook and Umpqua National Forests.

PUERTO RICO

Caribbean National Forest – On January 17, 1903, President Roosevelt established the Louquillo National Forest. In 1935, its name was changed to Caribbean. This forest has the duel distinction of being the only tropical rain forest in the U.S. National Forest System and the smallest forest at 28,000 acres. What it lacks in size, it makes up for in beauty and diversity.

SOUTH DAKOTA

Black Hills National Forest – On March 1, 1907, President Roosevelt established the Bear Lodge National Forest. After several consolidations and name changes, the former Bear Lodge is now part of the Black Hills National Forest. Cause of much strife between settlers and plains Indians, the mystical Black Hills rise from the harsh Dakota prairies. The forest is a blend of plains and Rocky Mountain vegetation. The Black Hills National Forest can be viewed from the Spearfish Canyon Scenic Byway and the Peter Nor Scenic Byway.

UTAH

Ashley National Forest – This 1.4-million-acre forest in northeast Utah and a portion of Wyoming includes the 276,000-acre High Unitas Wilderness. Dominant features include Kings Peak and Flaming Gorge. President Roosevelt established Ashley on July 1, 1908.

Dixie National Forest – President Roosevelt established Dixie September 25, 1905. Dixie is characteristic of Utah with its canyons and washed and bleached red sandstone. This 2-million acre forest has hundreds of miles of trails.

Fishlake National Forest – Three Roosevelt-established national forests have been consolidated with Fishlake:

Beaver Forest, Fillmore, and Glenwood. Fishlake has 1.8 million acres.

Wasatch-Cache National Forest – The Wasatch-Cache is where trappers would hide their cache of furs while they completed their trapping. This 1.2-million-acre forest near a gap in the Wasatch Mountains in northern Utah and southern Wyoming was designated by President Roosevelt in 1906 to protect a major watershed in this dry state.

Manti-La Sal National Forest – This southeastern Utah forest is a charming combination of mountain, desert, and canyon. A dominant feature is the LaSal Range with its 12,000-foot peaks. Its principal components were the Manti National Forest, established by President Roosevelt on May 29, 1903, and the La Sal National Forest, established on January 25, 1906.

WASHINGTON

Colville National Forest – In the northeast corner of Washington, Colville National Forest stretches from the western foothills of the Rockies to the Kettle and Selkirk Mountains to the west. President Roosevelt established this forest on March 1, 1907.

Gifford Pinchot National Forest – The Columbia National Forest was established by President Roosevelt on July 1, 1908. The name was changed to honor Gifford Pinchot in 1949. Gifford Pinchot National Forest is home to Mt. St. Helens. Located in southwest Washington, the forest embraces 1,3 million acre.

WYOMING

Medicine Bow National Forest – The Medicine Bow National Forest cuts an oblique swath from northeast Wyoming to south central Wyoming and into Colorado. Its rugged mountain terrain characterizes this 2.2 million acre Forest. President Roosevelt established Medicine Bow on May 22, 1902. It now contains the Sierra Madre National Forest first established in 1906.

Bridger-Teton National Forest – Teton National Forest was established July 1, 1908. It was combined with Bridger in 1973. Located immediately adjacent to Yellowstone and Teton National Parks, it is rich with rare plants and exotic wildlife.

Breathtaking; isn't it?

National Parks and Monuments

The end of the 1800s saw rising interest in the art and culture of American Indians and commensurate vandalism of and collection from ancient Indian sites, including the cliff dwellings and Pueblo ruins of the American southwest. Many of the historic areas were on public land. The federal government had no program to prevent amateur artifact collection (derisively called "pot hunting") or even simple vandalism. Following the Philadelphia Centennial Exhibition in 1876, "people without academic qualifications began excavating, as well, selling the recovered artifacts. Often, excavations entailed the destruction of the architecture as well as stratigraphy, with walls being pushed down in search for buried pots, tools, --- and mummies, which seemed to have especially popular appeal."[118] By the turn of the century, few historic Indian sites had been spared.

In 1906, Congress passed the Act for the Preservation of American Antiquities. President Roosevelt signed it into law on June 8, 1906. The Antiquities Act gave the President authority to declare and set aside for protection government-owned lands with "historic landmarks, historic and prehistoric structures, and other objects of historic or scientific interest." Roosevelt established 18 of these.

Occasionally, this designation was to secure immediate protection while the long term means and bounds of protection were determined.[119] Indeed, one out of every four national parks began as a national monument. Eventually, Roosevelt designations of Cinder Cone, Lassen Peak, Grand Canyon, and Mount Olympus National Monuments were designated national parks. Chaco Canyon National Monument subsequently became Chaco Culture National Historic Park.

Roosevelt was also an advocate of preservation through a system of parks:

> In addition, however, to this economic use of the wilderness, selected portions of it have been kept here and there in a state of nature, not merely for the sake of preserving the forests and the water, but for the sake of preserving all its beauties and wonders unspoiled by greedy and short-sighted vandalism. What has been accomplished in the Yellowstone Park affords the best possible object-lesson as to the desirability and practicability of establishing such wilderness reserves."[120]

Unlike monuments, refuges, and national forests, which Roosevelt could designate unilaterally, creation of parks required the cooperation of Congress. Congress set aside the first national park, Yellowstone, in 1872 in the Wyoming and Montana territories. Four more national parks were established by the time Roosevelt took office – Sequoia in California, Yosemite in California, General Grant in California, and Mount Rainier in Washington. A sixth park, Mackinac Island was established in 1875 but given back to Michigan in 1895.

Partly through Roosevelt's efforts, the number of national parks doubled during his administration: Crater Lake in Oregon; Wind Cave in South Dakota; Sully's Hill in North Dakota (this became the National Game Preserve in 1914); Platt in Oklahoma (now part of the Chickasaw National Recreation Area); and Mesa Verde in Colorado.

In addition, President Roosevelt played a role in establishing Yosemite National Park in its present form. In 1890, Congress created Yosemite National Park, a doughnut shaped park circling the Yosemite Valley. Lincoln had ceded the Valley to California in 1864. In 1905, the valley was given back to the federal government and Roosevelt worked to have it incorporated into the national park.

CRATER LAKE NATIONAL PARK

Oregon

Crater Lake is a brilliant blue lake in the Cascade Mountain range. Lying in a volcanic basin, the lake is five miles in diameter and ringed by sheer cliffs. Roosevelt signed the law creating Crater Lake National Park May 22, 1902. Crater Lake was "set apart as a public park or pleasuring ground for the benefit of the people."

WIND CAVE NATIONAL PARK

South Dakota

Wind Cave is in the Black Hills of South Dakota. A hunter who heard a strange whistling sound, which turned out to be air rushing through a 10-inch hole in the ground, discovered the cave in 1881. Excavations revealed one of the longest and most complex caves in the world. President Roosevelt signed the law creating Wind Cave National Park on January 9, 1903.

SULLY'S HILL NATIONAL PARK

North Dakota

In 1904, Congress set aside 900 acres and authorized the President to establish a public park. On June 2, 1904, he created the Sully's Hill National Park. In 1914, Sully's Hill was designated Sully's Hill National Game Preserve. It is described as "[r]olling glacial moraine hills on the south shore of Devils Lake, featuring mature mixed hardwood forest, native grassland, and brushland." 121 Today, Sully's Hill has established herds of bison and elk.

MESA VERDE NATIONAL PARK

Colorado

After several unsuccessful efforts, Congress passed legislation establishing Mesa Verde National Park in 1906. The legislation expressly directed the Secretary of the Interior to preserve from injury "the ruins and other works and relics of prehistoric primitive man" within the park. Theodore Roosevelt signed this legislation on May 26, 1906. The 52,000-acre park has 600 cliff dwellings and thousands of other archeological sites left by Indians who inhabited this area of southwest Colorado from the 400s to the 1200s.

PLATT NATIONAL PARK

Oklahoma

On June 29, 1906, the Sulphur Springs Reservation (purchased from the Choctaw and Chickasaw Nations in 1902) was designated the Platt National Park by a joint resolution of the Senate and House of Representatives. The park was designated because of the supposed healing properties of the sulfur, iron, and bromide springs. In 1976, it became part of the Chickasaw National Recreation Area.

DEVILS TOWER NATIONAL MONUMENT

Wyoming

Devils Tower National Monument was the first monument established by President Roosevelt. It was designated on September 24, 1906, after an unsuccessful effort in Congress to make it a national park. Devils Tower

National Monument is believed to be the center of an eroded volcano. In Roosevelt's presidential proclamation, Devils Tower was described as "an extraordinary example of the effect of erosion in the higher mountains." The present monument covers 1,347 acres.

The tower has cultural and religious significance to Indian tribes who call it the Bear's Lodge. According to Indian tradition, a grizzly bear's claws left the prominent vertical lines on the tower.

EL MORONATIONAL MONUMENT

New Mexico

El Moro National Monument, also known as Inscription Rock, is an ancient graffiti site. El Moro is a prominent sandstone feature that can be seen for great distances. Because of the solitary pool of water at El Moro's base, it became a destination for travelers in arid New Mexico. Its soft sandstone was easily carved, and it became a place for travelers to leave inscriptions. Anasazi, Spanish explorers, Civil War soldiers, and settlers all left messages - hundreds of inscriptions on El Moro. It was designated a national monument by Roosevelt on December 8, 1906.

YOSEMITE NATIONAL PARK

California

In 1864, President Lincoln signed legislation giving the Yosemite Valley to California. The ceded land was fifteen miles long and one mile wide and the grant was given for the express purpose of preservation and use as a park. The valley is of such beauty that the eloquent John Muir found it difficult to describe: "To describe the park in words is a hopeless task. The leanest sketch of each feature would need a whole chapter. Nor would any amount of space, however industriously scribbled, be of much avail."

In 1890, Congress set apart a forest reserve surrounding the Yosemite Valley. Although designated a forest reserve, the Congress treated it as a national park. On February 7, 1905, Congress added additional land and said the land would be known as Yosemite National Park. In 1905, California gave the valley back and the following year it was added to the Yosemite National Park.

PETRIFIED FOREST NATIONAL MONUMENT

Arizona

President Roosevelt designated this 90-square-mile monument on December 8, 1906 to protect the "mineralized remains of Mesozoic forests, commonly known as the 'Petrified Forest.'" The national monument contained one of the largest collections of petrified wood in the world – thousands of downed, petrified trees scattered over the desert floor. Included within the monument's boundaries are the Painted Desert and approximately 500 historic and archeological sites. In 1962, the monument was designated a national park.

MONTEZUMA CASTLE NATIONAL MONUMENT

Arizona

Montezuma Castle is a five-story Pueblo cliff dwelling above the Verde River valley floor. Early settlers incorrectly identified this structure as an Aztec ruin and dubbed it Montezuma's Castle. However, it was built by the Sinagua Indians who farmed the land in the 12th through 14th centuries. President Roosevelt designated the 840-acre Montezuma Castle National Monument on December 8, 1906.

CHACO CANYON NATIONAL MONUMENT

New Mexico

President Roosevelt's fifth designated national monument was Chaco Canyon National Monument, March 11, 1907. Renamed Chaco Culture National Historic Park in 1980, it contains up to a dozen large structures connected with as many as 74 outlying structures by good roads. The community was built and occupied by the Anasazi from around 850 A.D. through 1125. No one knows why the structures were built but they were big, spectacular, and important. According to the U.S. Park Service's printable travel guide: "Chaco Canyon was a major center of ancestral Puebloan culture between AD 850 and 1250. It was a hub of ceremony, trade, and administration for the prehistoric Four Corners area – unlike anything before or since."

LASSEN PEAK & CINDER CONE NATIONAL MONUMENTS

California

Representatives of Lassen and Plumas Counties, California, petitioned President Roosevelt to use the Antiquities Act to protect the volcanoes in those counties. On May 6, 1907, President Roosevelt designated two new monuments, Cinder Cone and Lassen Peak.

Cinder Cone National Monument was designated as an illustration "of volcanic activity which are of special importance in tracing the volcanic phenomena of that vicinity." The Lassen Peak proclamation identified the Lassen Peak National Monument of the "southern terminus of the long line of extinct volcanoes in the Cascade Range from which one of the greatest volcanic fields in the world extends." As a result of the national interest generated by subsequent eruptions, Lassen Peak and Cinder Cone

National Monuments were consolidated with additional land to form a new 150-square-mile park, Lassen Volcanic National Park.

GILA CLIFF DWELLINGS NATIONAL MONUMENT

New Mexico

President Roosevelt declared the Gila Cliff Dwelling National Monument on November 16, 1907. This 533-acre monument is located in the Gila National Forest and at the edge of the nation's first wilderness area – the Gila Wilderness. People of the Mogollon culture inhabited the area from approximately 1280 through the early 1300s. Mogollons were concentrated within 100 miles of what is now the New Mexico - Arizona line and as far south as Chihuahua and Sonora in Mexico. They were an agrarian people whose distinct culture began around 300 AD.

TONTO NATIONAL MONUMENT

Arizona

President Roosevelt designated Tonto National Monument on December 19, 1907, to protect "two prehistoric ruins of ancient cliff dwellings ... of great ethnographic, scientific, and educational interest." The Salado Indians, farmers, hunters, and gatherers who inhabited the Tonto basin from 1150 through 1450, made these well-preserved dwellings. The Tonto National Monument contains the only example of prehistoric Salado culture in the national park system. In addition to the two main dwellings which were the impetus for the designation, 13 smaller dwellings have been found within the monument.

MUIR WOODS NATIONAL MONUMENT

California

In 1903, President Roosevelt visited Yosemite with John Muir. Muir reportedly pushed the President to use his influence to preserve California's magnificent redwood and sequoia trees. Roosevelt got an opportunity in 1908. Congressman and Mrs. William Kent gave the federal government 295 acres of old-growth redwoods. President Roosevelt promptly designated (January 19, 1908) this acreage as Muir Woods National Monument ensuring the survival of the trees that grow up to 250 feet and 12 feet in diameter.

GRAND CANYON NATIONAL MONUMENT

Arizona

President Roosevelt visited the Grand Canyon in 1903. It had a profound impact on him, and several times he asked Congress to make it a national park. However, park status was not in the offing. This, of course, did not stop Roosevelt. On January 11, 1908, Roosevelt designated 800,000 acres of the Grand Canyon as a national monument; under the terms of the Antiquities Act, this was the "smallest area compatible with proper care and management of the objects to be protected." In 1916, the Grand Canyon National Monument was designated a national park. Its boundaries have been expanded since the original designation.

PINNACLES NATIONAL MONUMENT

California

In central California is Pinnacles National Monument. It takes its name from towering rock spires.

Pinnacles National Monument was designated on January 16, 1908. When designated, Pinnacles National Monument was 2,060 acres; its boundaries have been increased five times by presidents and once by Congress to its present size - 24,500 acres.

The monument is characterized by the effects of millions of years of erosion and the shifting San Andreas Fault: spires, massive monoliths, domes, caves, talus passages, sheer walled canyons, and subterranean passages. Within the monument is a designated wilderness area. The monument also serves as a breeding area for the endangered California condor.

JEWEL CAVE NATIONAL MONUMENT

South Dakota

Jewel Cave, in the Black Hills of South Dakota, is named for the calcite crystals found within almost every chamber of this extensive cave. Jewel Cave, discovered in 1900, is the third longest cave in the world. Roosevelt designated the cave a national monument on February 7, 1908. The current monument contains 1,274 acres.

NATURAL BRIDGES NATIONAL MONUMENT

Utah

Natural Bridges National Monument was designated by President Roosevelt on April 16, 1908 to protect a "number of natural bridges situated in southeastern Utah having heights more lofty and spans far greater than any heretofore known to exist." The bridges are outstanding examples of erosion. Although the Natural Bridges National Monument was designated for this limited purpose, it was twice expanded to incorporate prehistoric ruins. Today, the monument protects the natural bridges, historic ruins, an outstanding canyon system, and beautiful views.

TUMACACORI NATIONAL MONUMENT

Arizona

Tumacacori is one settlement within a chain of Spanish missions that once stretched from Sonora, Mexico to Tucson, Arizona. A series of Spanish churches was constructed at Tumacacori beginning in 1691. The Franciscan church, which is the beneficiary of monument status, was built in 1822. The priests were driven away by Apaches and the mission fell to ruin. On September 15, 1908, President Roosevelt designated nine acres around the mission as the Tumacacori National Monument. Remains of the 1691 Jesuit mission also are within the protected site. In 1990, the boundaries were enlarged to include two more missions and the designation was changed to Tumacacori National Historic Park.

WHEELER NATIONAL MONUMENT

Colorado

Wheeler was "discovered" by Frank Spencer, Supervisor of the Rio Grande National Forest in 1907. Wheeler National Monument was designated on December 7, 1908 to protect "volcanic formations ... of unusual scientific interest as illustrating erratic erosion." For many years, few visited the monument because of its inaccessibility. In 1950, monument status of Wheeler was revoked and the land was transferred to the Forest Service. It now is maintained as part the Wheeler Geologic Area within the Rio Grande National Forest.

MOUNT OLYMPUS NATIONAL MONUMENT

Washington

President Roosevelt designated Mount Olympus National Monument on March 2, 1909, just two days before leaving office. The designation included 600,000 acres within the 2-million acre Olympic National Forest. The stated reasons for the designation were scientific interest in its glaciers and Olympic elk, also known as Roosevelt elk. In 1937, President Franklin D. Roosevelt secured national park status and expanded its boundaries. In 1988, 95 percent of the park was designated "wilderness," thereby securing added protection against encroachment. Today, Olympic National Park contains three distinct environments: glacier-capped mountains, old-growth temperate rain forest, and coastal beaches. Within the park are the summer range and breeding grounds of the Roosevelt elk.

LEWIS AND CLARK CAVERN NATIONAL MONUMENT

Montana

President Roosevelt established the Lewis and Clark Cavern National Monument on May 11, 1908. The limestone cavern, 600 feet long and 400 feet deep, overlooks the Lewis and Clark Trail along the Jefferson River. The cave eventually was closed because of vandalism and lack of funding to properly protect it. In 1937, the national monument listing was abolished.

National Wildlife Refuges

From an early age, Roosevelt had a vigorous interest in wildlife and wild places. He had a "naturalist's instincts, and [a]...genuine love of all forms of wild life." [122] As early as 7, Teedie, as he was then called, was measuring a dead seal near a Broadway market and recording the information in his journal.[123] He always was collecting, and measuring, and recording. Author Nathan Miller described how Roosevelt returned from a collecting excursion; with pockets full, the only place for the transport of the frogs was under his hat. Upon "meeting Mrs. Hamilton Fish on a streetcar, he politely lifted his hat and several frogs leaped to the floor."[124] Another time, "the Roosevelts' cook was horrified to find a dead mouse in the icebox, a specimen placed there by Teedie for preservation until needed for one of his experiments. 'Oh the loss to science,' he mourned after the mouse was thrown out. 'Oh, the loss.'"[125]

Young Roosevelt was a voracious reader and consumed numerous books about wildlife. His reading and collecting were augmented by the gift of a gun and taxidermy lessons. Forever more, Roosevelt was addicted to hunting and specimen collecting, and measuring and recording. He became an accomplished and renowned nature writer. Among the 24 books he authored are: *Hunting Trips of a Ranchman; Ranch Life and the Hunting Trail; The Wilderness Hunter; Outdoor Pastimes of an American Hunter; Good Hunting; African Game Trails; A Book-Lover's Holidays in the Open;* and *Life-Histories of African Game Animals.* Numerous magazine articles supplemented this writing. In 1887, he co-founded the Boone and Crockett Club to promote hunting, conservation, and vigorous enforcement of the game laws.

Roosevelt's love of wildlife extended well beyond what was hunted and stuffed or eaten, as demonstrated by this passage from his autobiography:

When I was President, we owned a little house in western Virginia; a delightful house, to us at least, although only a shell of rough boards. We used sometimes to go there in the fall, perhaps at Thanksgiving, and on these occasions we would have quail and rabbits of our own shooting, and once in a while a wild turkey. We also went there in the spring. Of course many of the birds were different from our Long Island friends. There were mocking-birds, the most attractive of all birds, and blue grosbeaks, and cardinals and summer redbirds, instead of scarlet tanagers, and those wonderful singers the Bewick's wrens, and the Carolina wrens. All these I was able to show John Burroughs when he came to visit us; although by the way, he did not appreciate as much as we did one set of inmates of the cottage – the flying squirrels. We loved having the flying squirrels, father and mother and half-grown young, in their nest among the rafters; and at night we slept so soundly that we did not in the least mind the wild gambols of the little fellows through the rooms, even when as sometimes happened, they would swoop down to the bed and scuttle across it. [126]

It is not surprising that Roosevelt created what is now know as the National Wildlife Refuge System. At the beginning of the 1900s, wildlife, particularly birds, was slaughtered for various reasons – market hunting of fowl for food, collection and sale of eggs, collection of plumes and feathers for the millinery trade, and sport. Roosevelt's speeches and writings constantly assailed what he called "greed and wantonness" of those who ravaged America's wildlife.

Roosevelt always gave credit to the Audubon Society for pioneering the wildlife refuge system. At the urging of the Florida Audubon Society, President Roosevelt designated the first National Wildlife Refuge, Pelican Island. Fifty more would follow during his presidency along with four national game preserves.

Even though Roosevelt achieved monumental accomplishments in forest and water conservation, protecting wildlife seemed to make him most proud. In his autobiography, he detailed the important "steps to preserve from destruction beautiful and wonderful wild creatures whose existence was threatened by greed and wantonness. During the seven and a half years closing on March 4, 1909, more was accomplished for the protection of wild life in the United States than during all of the previous years, excepting only the creation of Yellowstone National Park." [127]

Of particular significance to Roosevelt were his efforts to protect American bison. Only six years before becoming president, he lamented:

> Gone forever are the mighty herds of the lordly buffalo. A few solitary individuals and small bands are still to be found scattered here and there in the wilder parts of the plains; and though most of these will be very soon destroyed, others will for some years fight off their doom and lead a precarious existence either in remote and almost desert portions of the country near the Mexican frontier, or else in the wildest and most inaccessible fastness of the Rocky Mountains; but the great herds, that for the first three quarters of this century

formed the distinguishing and characteristic feature of the Western plains, have vanished forever.[128]

His concern was understandable. At the beginning of the 19th century, an estimated 60 million bison roamed North America. By the time of Roosevelt's birth, bison were gone east of the Mississippi. By the time Roosevelt was sworn into office, bison were almost extinct. Two wild herds remained, one in Canada and one in Yellowstone Park. The total bison population was estimated at 1,000. Therefore, it was with pleasure that he recounted in his autobiography the following accomplishments:

> The securing in 1902 of the first appropriation for the preservation of buffalo and the establishment in the Yellowstone National Park of the first and now the largest herd of buffalo belonging to the government.

> The passage of the Act of January 24, 1905, creating the Wichita Game Preserves, In 1907, 12,000 acres of this preserve were enclosed with a woven wire fence for the reception of the herd of fifteen buffalo donated by the New York Zoological Society.

* * *

> The passage of the Act of May 23, 1908, providing for the establishment of the National Bison Range in Montana.[129]

Today, the bison herds have increased. The North America population is approximately 200,000. Wildlife refuges created by Roosevelt (or by Congress with Roosevelt's signature) with present-day bison herds include National Bison Range, 370 to 500 bison; Sully's Hill

National Game Preserve, 173 to 380 bison; and Wichita Mountains National Wildlife Refuge, 480 to 575 bison. In addition, the Yellowstone herd, for which money was first appropriated in 1902, stands at 2,000 to 3,500. Government herds are also maintained at Fort Niobara National Wildlife Refuge (350 to 490), National Elk Refuge (173 to 380), Neal Smith National Wildlife Refuge (35), Badlands National Park (350 to 440), and Theodore Roosevelt National Park (415 to 450).

Twice, Roosevelt dispatched military forces to protect wildlife. In 1903, Roosevelt issued an executive order placing Midway Atoll under U.S. control. The order was intended, in part, to provide a basis to stop the "wanton destruction [by Japanese fishermen] of birds that breed on Midway" for their feathers and eggs. In 1904, Roosevelt dispatched 21 marines to Midway to enforce his order. Military forces were again dispatched in 1907. This time, the purpose would be to stop the ruthless slaughter of Pribilof fur seals by Japanese.

President Roosevelt issued several executive orders protecting various islands in the Bering Sea and Aleutian Island chain, including a National Bird Reservation on the Pribilof Islands. Executive Order 1049, creating the Bogoslof Islands National Wildlife Refuge in Alaska, is indicative of Roosevelt's desire to stop "wanton destruction." That order states, in part:

It is unlawful for any person to hunt, trap, capture, willfully disturb or kill any bird of any kind whatever, or take eggs of such birds within the limits of this reservation....Warning is expressly given to all persons not to commit any acts herein enumerated and which are prohibited by law.

Similar language would eventually find its way into the Marine Mammal Protection Act and the Endangered Species Act.

The Klamath Lake National Wildlife refuge (now known as the Lower Klamath National Wildlife Refuge) was the first overlay refuge created wholly within a reclamation project. Seventeen overlay refuges were designated on a single day, February 25, 1909. Of the fifty-five refuges established during Roosevelt's presidency, 19 have been removed from specific federal protection. One was removed because it was a fragile barrier island and eroded away. A second may have been lost for similar reasons. Yet another was de-listed when it was discovered not to be on federally owned land. The vast majority of the de-listed refuges, however, were overlay refuges designated on February 25, 1909.

The remaining refuges provide an extraordinary segment of President Roosevelt's legacy. Lands of untold beauty, diversity, and ecological significance have been protected. Certain animal populations have rebounded, in part, because of these initial steps taken by Roosevelt toward wildlife preservation. For example, the beleaguered bird populations on the diminutive Farallon Islands (designated in February 1909) have soared; the Farallons now host the largest seabird rookery in the lower 48 states.

In addition to setting aside land, Roosevelt believed that wildlife must be preserved through wise laws and wise enforcement:

> Every believer in manliness, and therefore in manly sport, and every lover of nature, every man who appreciates the majesty and beauty of the wilderness and of the wild life, should strike hands with far-sighted men who wish to preserve our

material resources, in the effort to keep our forests, and our game beasts, game birds, and game fish – indeed, all the living creatures of the prairie, and woodland, and seashore – from wanton destruction.

Above all, we should realize that the effort toward this end is essentially a democratic movement. It is entirely in our power as a nation to preserve large tracts of wilderness, which are valueless for agricultural purposes and unfit for settlement, as playgrounds for rich and poor alike, and to preserve the game so that it shall continue to exist for the benefit of all lovers of nature.... But this can only be achieved by wise laws and by a resolute enforcement of the laws.[130]

From this leadership, the federal government and the states have committed themselves to wise laws for the benefit of wildlife. Today, the National Wildlife Refuge system is managed by the U.S. Fish and Wildlife Service in the Department of the Interior. The system has 93 million acres spread among more than 530 refuges dedicated to the protection and conservation of fish and wildlife.

PELICAN ISLANDNATIONAL WILDLIFE REFUGE

Florida, March 14, 1903

Pelican Island lies in the Indian River Lagoon. It straddles the line between the temperate and tropical zones. Thus, the refuge has temperate and tropical flora and fauna, making it biologically diverse. Among the nesting species are brown pelicans, wood storks, various egrets and herons, and the common moorhen. It is also an important nesting area for loggerhead and green sea turtles. President Roosevelt enlarged the sanctuary on January 26, 1909 to include several adjacent islands. Today, it also is designated a National Historic Landmark and a wilderness area.

BRETON ISLAND NATIONAL WILDLIFE REFUGE

Louisiana, October 4, 1904

Breton Island is an island in the Chandeleur chain - a series of barrier islands located in the Gulf of Mexico. Other islands were added to the refuge and it now is known as the Breton National Wildlife Refuge. Numerous sea birds use the refuge. Nesting species include approximately 10,000 brown pelicans as well as piping plovers, laughing gulls, and various terns (royal, Caspian, and least). In 1975, 1,000 acres in this 5,000-acre refuge were designated wilderness. Shallow bays and warm waters enhance the food production in the area and, thus, the value of the habitat resource.

STUMP LAKE NATIONAL WILDLIFE REFUGE

North Dakota, March 9, 1905

In the 1890s, Stump Lake, North Dakota, was an important breeding ground for migratory waterfowl. It also was a popular hunting area. In 1905, President Roosevelt designated five islands (28 acres) within Stump Lake as a national bird reservation. It is a major staging area for migrating canvasback ducks in the fall. Tundra swans and snow geese also have been sighted there.

WICHITA NATIONAL GAME PRESERVE

Oklahoma, June 5, 1905

This refuge was the first of four game preserves established during the Roosevelt presidency. It is now known as the Wichita Mountains National Wildlife Refuge.

When established, it was bereft of buffalo. Restocking first occurred in 1907 after Congress appropriated money to fence a major portion of the preserve. Originally, the New York Zoological Society donated 15 bison. Today, herds of bison, elk, deer, and long horned cattle are preserved on Wichita's 59,000 acres.

SISKIWIT ISLANDS BIRD RESERVATION

Michigan, October 10, 1905

The Siskiwit Islands are near Isle Royale in Lake Superior, Michigan. In 1931, the reservation was incorporated into the Isle Royale National Park. In 1973, the Park attained wilderness designation. Isle Royale National Park hosts wolf and moose populations and is home to the most stable loon population in Michigan.

HURON ISLANDS NATIONAL WILDLIFE REFUGE

Michigan, October 10, 1905

The Huron Islands National Wildlife Refuge, in Lake Superior, a 147-acre refuge, also is designated a wilderness area. Among bird populations are merlins and bald eagles.

PASSAGE KEY NATIONAL WILDLIFE REFUGE

Florida, October 10, 1905

Passage Key National Wildlife Refuge lies near the mouth of Tampa Bay. It now is part of the larger Chassahowitzka National Wildlife area. Over 50 species of birds regularly use Passage Key. Prominent are sandwich and royal terns. Laughing gulls, black skimmers, brown pelicans, and oyster catchers also nest there.

GRANDE CANYON NATIONAL GAME PRESERVE

Arizona, June 29, 1906

The Grand Canyon was a particular favorite of President Roosevelt - "wonderful and beautiful beyond description", a "desolate and awful sublimity." The Grand Canyon National Game Preserve lies along the North Rim of the Grand Canyon. The Kaibab Plateau is a haven for wildlife and contains some of Southwest's last remaining old growth forests. Among other things, it has populations of North Kaibab deer and bison. In 1906, a game preserve was established within the Grand Canyon National Forest. Two years later, Roosevelt added another layer of protection through designation of approximately 800,000 acres as a national monument.

SHELL KEYS NATIONAL WILDLIFE REFUGE

Louisiana, August 17, 1907

President Roosevelt described Shell Keys as "unsurveyed islets in the Gulf of Mexico about three and one-half miles south of Marsh Island, Louisiana." Now, because of erosion, only one islet exists. Nesting species include royal terns, sandwich terns, black skimmers, and laughing gulls.

THREE ARCH ROCKS NATIONAL WILDLIFE REFUGE

Oregon, October 14, 1907

This distinctive refuge and wilderness area consists of three rock islands (and several smaller rocks) with a total land mass of approximately 15 acres. It is part of the Oregon Coastal Refuge complex. During nesting season, Three Arch Rocks National Wildlife Refuge is home to about 200,000 common murres and 2,000 to 4,000 tufted puffins, an elusive bird that nests underground. California sea lions, harbor seals, bald eagles, peregrine falcons, and brown pelicans also use the site. The refuge is closed to all except researchers with permission.

FLATTERY ROCKS, COPALIS ROCKS, AND QUILLAYUTE NEEDLES NATIONAL WILDLIFE REFUGES

Washington, October 23, 1907

On October 23, 1907, President Roosevelt designated three separate rock, reef, and island groupings off the coast of Washington as national bird reservation. Flattery Rocks, Copalis Rocks, and Quillayute Needles are consolidated for certain management purposes into the Washington Islands National Wildlife Refuges, protecting approximately 486 acres. Added protection is ensured through wilderness designation for most of the Washington Islands National Wildlife Refuges. As noted in National Wildlife Service information, the Washington Islands National Wildlife Refuges provide significant protection for nearly 1 million coastal birds. The principal goal of the Washington Islands National Wildlife Refuges is the protection of migratory birds and other native wildlife with their associated habitats, with special emphasis on seabirds.

TORTUGAS KEYS NATIONAL BIRD RESERVATION

Florida, April 6, 1908

This reservation was composed of the Dry Tortugas in Florida, a cluster of islands made of coral and sand 70 miles west of Key West, Florida. Included in the designation were Loggerhead Key, Texas Rock, Sand Key, Middle Key, Iowa Rock, East Key, North Key, Bird Key, Bush Key, Long Key, and Garden Key. The Dry Tortugas are home to almost 200 species of rare birds. Included among the bird populations are sooty terns, brown noddy terns, brown boobies, double-crested cormorants, pelicans, and frigate birds.

In 1935, when President Franklin Roosevelt designated Dry Tortugas National Monument to protect Fort Jefferson, it appears that the refuge designation was eliminated. In 1992, the Dry Tortugas were designated a national park to better protect the historical and natural features.

NATIONAL BISON RANGE

Montana, May 23, 1908

Congress, on land purchased by the Roosevelt administration for this purpose, created the National Bison Range. It was the first time that land was purchased for wildlife protection. The range is home to approximately 450 bison. The 18,500-acre range also is home to elk, deer, bear, coyote, and more than 200 species of birds.

KEY WEST NATIONAL WILDLIFE REFUGE

Florida, August 8, 1908

This refuge is combined with three others to form the Florida Keys National Wildlife Refuges. The combined system contains 25,000 acres of land and the surrounding water. Nearly 300 species of birds use the mangrove islands and sandy beaches and dunes. The refuge also provides nesting areas for endangered Atlantic green, loggerhead, and hawksbill turtles.

KLAMATH LAKE NATIONAL WILDLIFE REFUGE

California & Oregon, August 8, 1908

The Klamath Lake National Wildlife Refuge, now known as the Lower Klamath National Wildlife Refuge, straddles the California – Oregon line. It was established in 1908 within an area previously set aside by the Roosevelt administration for reclamation. Over the years, the goals and objectives of a reclamation project (responsible for the loss of almost 80 percent of the surface water in the Klamath Basin) and the refuge have clashed.

Nevertheless, the refuge was designated "as a preserve and breeding ground for native birds" and it serves a vital function. Up to 80 percent of the birds using the Pacific flyway utilize the Lower Klamath National Wildlife Refuge and the other five National Wildlife Refuges in the Klamath Basin. The Lower Klamath National Wildlife Refuge is known for its winter concentration of bald eagles. Elk, pronghorn antelope, and black bears also are found in the refuge.

LAKE MALHEUR NATIONAL WILDLIFE REFUGE

Oregon, August 18, 1908

This vast lake and wetland area lies in Oregon's southeastern desert. The wetland, one of the largest in North America, is formed because water flows into the system, but not out. During spring migrations, approximately 250,000 ducks, 125,000 geese, and 6,000 lesser sandhill cranes use the refuge. Throughout the year, ducks, geese, shorebirds, and songbirds nest within the refuge. President Roosevelt designated 81,786 acres in 1908. Included were the shorelines of Lakes Malheur and Harney and the streams and waters connecting them. The refuge was expanded several times, including a 64,717 addition by President Franklin

Roosevelt in 1935. In 1940, the refuge's name was changed to Malheur National Wildlife Refuge.

CHASE LAKE NATIONAL WILDLIFE REFUGE

North Dakota, August 28, 1908

The 4,385-acre Chase Lake National Wildlife Refuge is located in the prairie pothole region of North Dakota, This region is a mixture of glacier formed ponds and lakes and prairie grasslands. Chase Lake is an alkali lake nestled amongst rolling prairie grasslands.

Although Chase Lake National Wildlife Refuge is an incredibly productive duck-breeding habitat, the refuge principally was created to protect native white pelicans. The white pelican population in the refuge now exceeds 20,000. Deer, fox, coyote, badger, and weasel also are common in the refuge. In 1975, most of Chase Lake National Wildlife Refuge was designated wilderness.

PINE ISLAND NATIONAL WILDLIFE REFUGE

Florida, September 15, 1908

MATLACHA PASS NATIONAL WILDLIFE REFUGE

Florida, September 26, 1908

ISLAND BAY NATIONAL WILDLIFE REFUGE

Florida, October 23, 1908

These three refuges are comprised of many islands around Sanibel Island along Florida's west coast. Many birds including herons, pelicans, egrets, ibis, and cormorants use the refuges. West Indian manatees, wood storks, eastern indigo snakes, American crocodiles, and bald eagles also frequent the area. The refuges are incorporated within a larger State of Florida Aquatic Preserve. The Audubon Guide to the National Wildlife Refuges-Southeast advises that "[v]igorous mosquito populations help to protect the wildlife on the islands."[131]

HAWAIIAN ISLANDS NATIONAL WILDLIFE REFUGE

Hawaii, February 3, 1909

The Hawaiian Islands National Wildlife Refuge was a chain of coral reefs and atolls stretching for 800 miles from the north west of Hawaii. Millions of birds use the refuge; among birds using the refuge are Laysana albatross and the black-footed albatross. The endangered Hawaiian monk seal also is dependant upon this refuge. President Clinton expanded the refuge and recently Congress incorporated the refuge into a much larger National Wildlife Hawaiian Islands Coral Reef Reserve.

DEER FLAT NATIONAL WILDLIFE REFUGE

Idaho, February 25, 1909

Deer Flat National Wildlife Refuge is one of the 17 overlay refuges designated by President Roosevelt on February 25, 1909. It was designated along a portion of Lake Lowell, a Bureau of Reclamation Lake in Idaho. Lake Lowell continues to be maintained as part of a reclamation project in the Boise River Valley. In 1963, Deer Flat was combined with the Snake River Migratory Waterfowl Refuge. The combined refuge now encompasses the entire periphery of Lake Lowell. The refuge is an important habitat for ducks and geese. Numerous species of owls nest at Deer Flat including burrowing, long-eared, short-eared, northern saw-whet, western screech, barn, and great horned owls.

COLD SPRINGS NATIONAL WILDLIFE REFUGE

Oregon, February 25, 1909

Cold Springs National Wildlife Refuge is contained within a Bureau of Reclamation project, situated and saturated in northeast Oregon. The 3,117-acre refuge is a principal destination for geese and ducks. The refuge is a combination of open water, marsh, sagebrush, and grasslands. Five species of sandpiper (lesser, western, spotted, solitary, and semi-palmated) use this refuge during a portion of the year. The uplands provide habitat for coyotes and bobcats.

PATHFINDER NATIONAL WILDLIFE REFUGE

Wyoming, February 25, 1909

Pathfinder National Wildlife Refuge is a portion of the Bureau of Reclamation's Pathfinder Reservoir. Open water and/or mud flats and sagebrush and grasslands characterize the refuge.

MINDOKA NATIONAL WILDLIFE REFUGE

Idaho, February 25, 1909

Gulls, terns, grebes, herons, egrets, ducks and geese abound in the Snake River Valley's Mindoka National Wildlife Refuge. Also frequent are bald and golden eagles. White pelicans nest in the refuge. Tundra swan appear during migrations. A Bureau of Reclamation lake supports the 20,721-acre Refuge.

TUXEDNI NATIONAL WILDLIFE REFUGE

Alaska, February 27, 1909

Roosevelt designated two islands in Tuxedni Bay, Duck Island and Chisik Island. Tuxedni was established as a refuge for sea birds, bald eagles, and peregrine falcons. In 1970, the refuge became incorporated with a wilderness area. In 1980 it became a subunit of the Gulf of Alaska Unit of the 4.9-million-acre Alaska Maritime National Wildlife Refuge.

SAINT LAZARIA NATIONAL WILDLIFE REFUGE

Alaska, February 25, 1909

Saint Lazaria National Wildlife Refuge is a 65-acre sanctuary in Sitka Sound on Alaska's southern panhandle. In 1970 it was designated a wilderness area. In 1980 it became a subunit of the Gulf of Alaska Unit of the Alaska Maritime National Wildlife Refuge. Over a half a million birds nest in the refuge including petrels, tufted puffins, and rhinoceros auklets. Also present are pigeon guillemots, common murres, glaucous-winged gulls, and pelagic cormorants.

YUKON DELTA NATIONAL WILDLIFE REFUGE

Alaska, February 25, 1909

This massive refuge contains the deltas of the Yukon and Kuskokwim Rivers in western Alaska. "This is a land of *greats*. Great salmon runs, several million shore birds and waterfowl, hundreds of thousands of lakes and ponds, and two of America's greatest rivers, the Yukon and the Kuskokwim."[132] This treeless refuge of low-lying marsh, lakes, ponds, and streams is home to millions of water birds. Moose, caribou, musk ox (introduced), bear, and wolves also are found in the refuge. Two wilderness areas within the land provide an extra layer of protection.

CULEBRA NATIONAL WILDLIFE REFUGE

Puerto Rico, February 25, 1909

Culebra National Wildlife Refuge is a 1,568-acre sanctuary consisting of Culebra Island and 22 smaller islands. The objective of the refuge is to protect and manage significant seabird colonies, and endangered marine turtles, as well as tropical native vegetation. The refuge's diverse habitat of mangroves, open water, grasslands, and subtropical forest enable it to host thousands of birds. Included among the bird species are laughing gulls, bridled terns, sooty terns, brown noddys, masked and red-footed boobies, and roseate terns. Endangered hawksbill, Atlantic green, leatherback, and Atlantic loggerhead turtles are found in the Refuge.

Today, Culebra is combined with seven other National Wildlife Refuges to form the Caribbean Islands National Wildlife Refuges.

FARALLON NATIONAL WILDLIFE REFUGE

California, February 25, 1909

The Farallon Islands are small rocks rising above the sea off the coast of California, approximately 28 miles from San Francisco. In 1909, President Roosevelt designated the Middle Farallon and the North Farallons a national bird reservation. In 1969 the 70-acre Southeast Farallon Islands were added bringing the refuge to 211 acres. Despite their diminutive size, the Farallons are productive, hosting the largest sea bird colony in the lower 48 states. Approximately 400,00 birds populate the islands – black oyster catchers, pigeon guillemots, cormorants (double-crested, pelagic, and

Brandt's), murres, auklets, and puffins. Elephant seals and sea lions also populate the Farallons.

BEHRING SEA, PRIBILOF, FIRE ISLAND, and BOGOSLOF NATIONAL WILDLIFE REFUGES

Alaska, February 27, 1909; March 2, 1909

In the waning days of his administration, President Roosevelt designated Bering Sea, Pribilof, and Bogoslof National Bird Reserves and the Fire Island Game Preserve. Fire Island was a new volcano in the Bogoslof group in the Aleutian Islands. All are now part of the Alaska Maritime National Wildlife Refuge, a sprawling sanctuary of over 2,400 islands, rocks, islets, and reefs. The 4.5-million-acre refuge is home to millions of birds and numerous marine mammals including walrus, sea otters, seals, and sea lions.

DE-LISTED REFUGES

INDIAN KEY NATIONAL WILDLIFE REFUGE

Florida, February 10, 1906

This refuge was revoked on June 26, 1950.

TERN ISLANDS NATIONAL WILDLIFE REFUGE

Louisiana, August 8, 1907

This refuge was de-listed on April 15, 1953 by Public Land Order 892.

EAST TIMBALIER ISLAND BIRD RESERVATION

Louisiana, December 7, 1907

Roosevelt described East Timbalier Island as "small marshy islands" in the Gulf of Mexico. It was de-listed as a National Wildlife Refuge in April 1969.

PALMA SOLA NATIONAL WILDLIFE REFUGE

Florida, September 26, 1908

The Palma Sola National Wildlife Refuge was an unsurveyed island in Palma Sola Bay, off the west coast of Florida. The island eroded away and Executive Order 942 revoked the designation on February 6, 1948.

LOCH-KATRINE NATIONAL WILDLIFE REFUGE

Wyoming, October 26, 1908

Loch-Katrine was de-listed on May 20, 1921.

MOSQUITO INLET NATIONAL BIRD RESERVATION

Florida, February 24, 1908

Mosquito Inlet National Bird Reservation was created among the "small mangrove and salt-grass islets, shoals, sandbars, and sand-spits in and near the mouths of the Halifax and Hillsboro Rivers" on Florida's east coast. Executive Order 4832 revoked the designation on March 17, 1928.

BELLE FOURCHE NATIONAL WILDLIFE REFUGE

South Dakota, February 25, 1909

The refuge was revoked in 1964 because of excessive recreational use and inadequate wildlife use.

STRAWBERRY VALLEY NATIONAL WILDLIFE REFUGE

Utah, February 25, 1909

The refuge was discontinued on March 16, 1961 when the land was transferred from the federal government and, therefore, a national wildlife refuge was no longer possible.

CONCONULLY NATIONAL WILDLIFE REFUGE

Washington, February 25, 1909

This refuge was revoked on March 31, 1960.

KEECHELUS NATIONAL WILDLIFE REFUGE

Washington, February 25, 1909

Executive Order 3468 revoked this refuge on May 20, 1921.

KACHESS NATIONAL WILDLIFE REFUGE

Washington, February 25, 1909

Executive Order 3468 revoked this refuge on May 20, 1921.

CLEALUM NATIONAL WILDLIFE REFUGE

Washington, February 25, 1909

Executive Order 3468 revoked this refuge on May 20, 1921.

BUMPING LAKE NATIONAL WILDLIFE REFUGE

Washington, February 25, 1909

Executive Order 3468 revoked this refuge on May 20, 1921.

SALT RIVER NATIONAL WILDLIFE REFUGE

Arizona, February 25, 1909

The Salt River National Wildlife Refuge was discontinued on March 21, 1961. Various other Refuges exist in the area as part of the Theodore Roosevelt Dam and Reclamation Project.

EAST PARK NATIONAL WILDLIFE REFUGE

California, February 25, 1909

This designation was revoked on May 20, 1921.

WILLOW CREEK NATIONAL WILDLIFE REFUGE

Montana, February 25, 1909

On May 29, 1968, this refuge was discontinued and the land transferred to the Bureau of Reclamation.

CARLSBAD NATIONAL WILDLIFE REFUGE

New Mexico, February 25, 1909

This designation was revoked by Executive Order 1032 on August 11, 1947

RIO GRANDE NATIONAL WILDLIFE REFUGE

New Mexico, February 25, 1909

The refuge was revoked by Executive Order in 1947.

SHOSHONE NATIONAL WILDLIFE REFUGE

Wyoming, February 25, 1909

Executive Order 3735 revoked this refuge on August 18, 1922.

ROOSEVELT SPEECHES AND OTHER COMMUNICATIONS[1]

First Annual Message to Congress
December 3, 1901

Public opinion throughout the United States has moved steadily toward a just appreciation of the value of forests, whether planted or of natural growth. The great part played by them in the creation and maintenance of the national wealth is now mournfully realized than ever before. Wise forest protection does not mean the withdrawal of forest resources, whether of wood, water, or grass, from contributing their full share to the welfare of the people, but, on the contrary, gives the assurance of larger and more certain supplies. The fundamental idea of forestry is the perpetuation of forests by use. Forest protection is not an end of itself; it is a means to increase and sustain the resources of our country and the industries which depend upon them. The preservation of our forests is an imperative business necessity. We have come to see clearly that whatever destroys the forest, except to make way for agriculture, threatens our well-being. The practical usefulness of the national forest reserves to the mining, grazing, irrigation, and other interests of the regions in which the reserves lie has led to a widespread demand by the people of the West for their protection and extension. The forest reserves will inevitably be of still greater use in the future than in the past. Additions should be made to them whenever practicable, and their usefulness should be increased by a thoroughly businesslike management. At present the protection of the forest reserves rests with the General Land Office, the mapping and

---

[1] The Annual Messages printed herein contain only Roosevelt's comments on conservation, reclamation, and public lands. The Special Messages to Congress also are edited.

description of their timber with the United States Geological Survey, and the preparation of plans for their conservative use with the Bureau of Forestry, which is also charged with the general advancement of practical forestry in the United States. These various functions should be united in the Bureau of Forestry, to which they properly belong. The present diffusion of responsibility is bad from every standpoint. It prevents that effective cooperation between the government and the men who utilize the resources of the reserves, without which the interests of both must suffer. The scientific bureaus generally should be put under the Department of Agriculture. The president should have by law the power of transferring lands for use as forest reserves to the Department of Agriculture. He already has such power in the case of lands needed by the departments of War and the Navy.

The wise administration of the forest reserves will be not less helpful to the interests which depend on water than to those which depend on wood and grass. The water supply itself depends upon the forest. In the arid region it is water, not land, which measures production. The western half of the United States would sustain a population greater than that of our whole country today if the waters that now run to waste were saved and used for irrigation. The forest and water problems are perhaps the most vital internal questions of the United States. Certain of the forest reserves should also be made preserves for the wild forest creatures. All of the reserves should be better protected from fires. Many of them need special protection because of the great injury done by livestock, above all by sheep. The increase in deer, elk, and other animals in the Yellowstone Park shows what may be expected when other mountain forests are properly protected by law and properly guarded. Some of these areas have been so denuded of surface vegetation by overgrazing that the ground breeding birds, including grouse and quail, and many mammals, including deer, have been exterminated or driven away. At the same time the water-storing capacity of the surface has been decreased or destroyed, thus promoting floods in times of rain and diminishing the flow of streams between rains.

In cases where natural conditions have been restored for a few years, vegetation has again carpeted the ground, birds and deer are coming back, and hundreds of persons, especially from the immediate neighborhood, come each summer to enjoy the privilege of camping. Some at least of the forest reserves should afford perpetual protection to the native fauna and flora, safe havens of refuge to our rapidly diminishing wild animals of the larger kinds, and free camping grounds for the ever-increasing numbers of men and women who have learned to find rest, health, and recreation in the splendid forests and flower-clad meadows of our mountains. The forest reserves should be set apart forever for the use and benefit of our people as a whole and not sacrificed to the shortsighted greed of a few. The forests are natural reservoirs. By restraining the streams in flood and replenishing them in drought they make possible the use of waters otherwise wasted. They prevent the soil from washing, and so protect the storage reservoirs from filling up with silt. Forest conservation is therefore an essential condition of water conservation. The forests alone cannot, however, fully regulate and conserve the waters of the arid region. Great storage works are necessary to equalize the flow of streams and to save the flood waters. Their construction has been conclusively shown to be an undertaking too vast for private effort. Nor can it be best accomplished by the individual states acting alone. Far-reaching interstate problems are involved; and the resources of single states would often be inadequate. It is properly a national function, at least in some of its features. It is as right for the national government to make the streams and rivers of the arid region useful by engineering works for water storage as to make useful the rivers and harbors of the humid region by engineering works of another kind. The storing of the floods in reservoirs at the headwaters of our rivers is but an enlargement of our present policy of river control, under which levees are built on the lower reaches of the same streams. The government should construct and maintain these reservoirs as it does other public works. Where their purpose is to regulate the flow of streams, the water should be turned freely into the channels in the dry season to take the same course under the same laws as the natural flow. The reclamation of the unsettled arid public lands presents a different problem. Here it is not enough to regulate the flow of streams. The object of the government is to dispose of the land to settlers who will build homes upon it. To accomplish this object water must be brought within their reach.

Second Annual Message to Congress

December 2, 1902

Few subjects of more importance have been taken up by the Congress in recent years than the inauguration of the system of nationally aided irrigation for the and regions of the far West. A good beginning therein has been made. Now that this policy of national irrigation has been adopted, the need of thorough and scientific forest protection will grow more rapidly than ever throughout the public-land States.

Legislation should be provided for the protection of the game, and the wild creatures generally, on the forest reserves. The senseless slaughter of game, which can by judicious protection be permanently preserved on our national reserves for the people as a whole, should be stopped at once. It is, for instance, a serious count against our national good sense to permit the present practice of butchering off such a stately and beautiful creature as the elk for its antlers or tusks.

So far as they are available for agriculture, and to whatever extent they may be reclaimed under the national irrigation law, the remaining public lands should be held rigidly for the home builder, the settler who lives on his land, and for no one else. In their actual use the desert-land law, the timber and stone law, and the commutation clause of the homestead law have been so perverted from the intention with which they were enacted as to permit the acquisition of large areas of the public domain for other than actual settlers and the consequent prevention of settlement. Moreover, the approaching exhaustion of the public ranges has of late led to much discussion as to the best manner of using these public lands in the West which are suitable chiefly or only for grazing. The sound and steady development of the West depends upon the building up of homes therein. Much of our prosperity as a nation has been due to the operation of the homestead law. On the other hand, we should recognize the fact that in the grazing region the man who corresponds to the homesteader may be unable to settle permanently if only allowed to use the same amount of pasture land that his brother, the homesteader, is allowed to use of arable land. One hundred and sixty acres of fairly rich and well-watered soil, or a much smaller amount of irrigated land, may keep a family in plenty, whereas no one could get a living from one hundred and sixty acres of dry pasture land capable of supporting at the outside only one head of cattle to every ten acres. In the past great tracts of the public domain have been fenced in by persons having no title thereto, in direct defiance of the law forbidding the maintenance or construction of any such unlawful enclosure of public land. For various reasons there has been little interference with such enclosures in the past, but ample notice has now been given the trespassers, and all the resources at the command of the Government will hereafter be used to put a stop to such trespassing.

In view of the capital importance of these matters, I commend them to the earnest consideration of the Congress, and if the Congress finds difficulty in dealing with them from lack of thorough knowledge of the subject, I recommend that provision be made for a commission of experts specially to investigate and report upon the complicated questions involved.

I especially urge upon the Congress the need of wise legislation for Alaska. It is not to our credit as a nation that Alaska, which has been ours for thirty-five years, should still have as poor a system of laws as is the case. No country has a more valuable possession in mineral wealth, in fisheries, furs, forests, and also in land available for certain kinds of farming and stockgrowing. It is a territory of great size and varied resources, well fitted to support a large permanent population. Alaska needs a good land law and such

Third Annual Message to Congress

December 7, 1903

I call your special attention to the Territory of Alaska. The country is developing rapidly, and it has an assured future. The mineral wealth is great and has as yet hardly been tapped. The fisheries, if wisely handled and kept under national control, will be a business as permanent as any other, and of the utmost importance to the people. The forests if properly guarded will form another great source of wealth. Portions of Alaska are fitted for farming and stock raising, although the methods must be adapted to the peculiar conditions of the country. Alaska is situated in the far north; but so are Norway and Sweden and Finland; and Alaska can prosper and play its part in the New World just as those nations have prospered and played their parts in the Old World. Proper land laws should be enacted; and the survey of the public lands immediately begun. Coal-land laws should be provided whereby the coal-land entryman may make his location and secure patent under methods kindred to those now prescribed for homestead and mineral entrymen. Salmon hatcheries, exclusively under Government control, should be established. The cable should be extended from Sitka westward. Wagon roads and trails should be built, and the building of railroads promoted in all legitimate ways. Light-houses should be built along the coast. Attention should be paid to the needs of the Alaska Indians; provision should be made for an officer, with deputies, to study their needs, relieve their immediate wants, and help them adapt themselves to the new conditions. The commission appointed to investigate, during the season of 1903, the condition and needs of the Alaskan salmon fisheries, has finished its work in the field, and is preparing a detailed report thereon. A preliminary report reciting the measures immediately required for the protection and preservation of the salmon industry has already been submitted to the Secretary of Commerce and Labor for his attention and for the needed action.

*   *   *

A gratifying disposition has been evinced by those having unlawful inclosures of public land to remove their fences. Nearly two million acres so inclosed have been thrown open on demand. In but comparatively few cases has it been necessary to go into court to accomplish this purpose. This work will be vigorously prosecuted until all unlawful inclosures have been removed. Experience has shown that in the western States themselves, as well as in the rest of the country, there is widespread conviction that certain of the public-land laws and the resulting administrative practice no longer meet the present needs. The character and uses of the remaining public lands differ widely from those of the public lands which Congress had especially in view when these laws were passed. The rapidly increasing rate of disposal of the public lands is not followed by a corresponding increase in home building. There is a tendency to mass in large holdings public lands, especially timber and grazing lands, and thereby to retard settlement. I renew and emphasize my recommendation of last year that so far as they are available for agriculture in its broadest sense, and to whatever extent they may be reclaimed under the national irrigation law, the remaining public lands should be held rigidly for the home builder. The attention of the Congress is especially directed to the timber and stone law, the desert-land law, and the commutation clause of the homestead law, which in their operation have in many respects conflicted with wise public-land policy. The discussions in the Congress and elsewhere have made it evident that there is a wide divergence of opinions between those holding opposite views on these subjects; and that the opposing sides have strong and convinced representatives of weight both within and without the Congress; the differences being not only as to matters of opinion but as to matters of fact. In order that definite information may be available for the use of the Congress, I have appointed a commission composed of W. A. Richards, Commissioner of the General Land Office; Gifford Pinchot, Chief of the Bureau of Forestry of the Department of Agriculture, and F. H. Newell, Chief Hydrographer of the Geological Survey, to report at the earliest practicable moment upon the condition, operation, and effect of the present land laws and on the use, condition, disposal, and settlement of the public lands. The commission will report especially what changes in organization, laws, regulations, and practice affecting the public lands are needed to effect the largest practicable disposition of the public lands to actual settlers who will build permanent homes upon them, and to secure in permanence the fullest and most effective use of the resources of the public lands; and it will make such other reports and recommendations as its study of these questions may suggest. The commission is to report immediately upon those points concerning which its judgment is clear; on any point upon which it has doubt it will take the time necessary to make investigation and reach a final judgment.

The work of reclamation of the arid lands of the West is progressing steadily and satisfactorily under the terms of the law setting aside the proceeds from the disposal of public lands. The corps of engineers known as the Reclamation Service, which is conducting the surveys and examinations, has been thoroughly organized, especial pains being taken to secure under the civil-service rules a body of skilled, experienced, and efficient men. Surveys and examinations are progressing throughout the arid States and Territories, plans for reclaiming works being prepared and passed upon by boards of engineers before approval by the Secretary of the Interior. In Arizona and Nevada, in localities where such work is pre-eminently needed, construction has already been begun. In other parts of the arid West various projects are well advanced towards the drawing up of contracts, these being delayed in part by necessities of reaching agreements or understanding as regards rights of way or acquisition of real estate. Most of the works contemplated for construction are of national importance, involving interstate questions or the securing of stable, self-supporting communities in the midst of vast tracts of vacant land. The Nation as a whole is of course the gainer by the creation of these homes, adding as they do to the wealth and stability of the country, and furnishing a home market for the products of the East and South. The reclamation law, while perhaps not ideal, appears at present to answer the larger needs for which it is designed. Further legislation is not recommended until the necessities of change are more apparent.

The study of the opportunities of reclamation of the vast extent of arid land shows that whether this reclamation is done by individuals, corporations, or the State, the sources of water supply must be effectively protected and the reservoirs guarded by the preservation of the forests at the headwaters of the streams. The engineers making the preliminary examinations continually emphasize this need and urge that the remaining public lands at the headwaters of the important streams of the West be reserved to insure permanency of water supply for irrigation. Much progress in forestry has been made during the past year. The necessity for perpetuating our forest resources, whether in public or private hands, is recognized now as never before. The demand for forest reserves has become insistent in the West, because the West must use the water, wood, and summer range which only such reserves can supply. Progressive lumbermen are striving, through forestry, to give their business permanence. Other great business interests are awakening to the need of forest preservation as a business matter. The Government's forest work should receive from the Congress hearty support, and especially support adequate for the protection of the forest reserves against fire. The forest-reserve policy of the Government has passed beyond the experimental stage and has reached a condition where scientific methods are essential to its successful prosecution. The administrative features of forest reserves are at present unsatisfactory, being divided between three Bureaus of two Departments. It is therefore recommended that all matters pertaining to forest reserves, except those involving or pertaining to land titles, be consolidated in the Bureau of Forestry of the Department of Agriculture.

Fourth Annual Message to Congress

December 6, 1904

During the two and a half years that have elapsed since the passage of the reclamation act rapid progress has been made in the surveys and examinations of the opportunities for reclamation in the thirteen States and three Territories of the arid West. Construction has already been begun on the largest and most important of the irrigation works, and plans are being completed for works which will utilize the funds now available. The operations are being carried on by the Reclamation Service, a corps of engineers selected through competitive civil-service examinations. This corps includes experienced consulting and constructing engineers as well as various experts in mechanical and legal matters, and is composed largely of men who have spent most of their lives in practical affairs connected with irrigation. The larger problems have been solved and it now remains to execute with care, economy, and thoroughness the work which has been laid out. All important details are being carefully considered by boards of consulting engineers, selected for their thorough knowledge and practical experience. Each project is taken up on the ground by competent men and viewed from the standpoint of the creation of prosperous homes, and of promptly refunding to the Treasury the cost of construction. The reclamation act has been found to be remarkably complete and effective, and so broad in its provisions that a wide range of undertakings has been possible under it. At the same time, economy is guaranteed by the fact that the funds must ultimately be returned to be used over again.

It is the cardinal principle of the forest-reserve policy of this Administration that the reserves are for use. Whatever interferes with the use of their resources is to be avoided by every possible means. But these resources must be used in such a way as to make them permanent. The forest policy of the Government is just now a subject of vivid public interest throughout the West and to the people of the United States in general. The forest reserves themselves are of extreme value to the present as well as to the future welfare of all the western public-land States. They powerfully affect the use and disposal of the public lands. They are of special importance because they preserve the water supply and the supply of timber for domestic purposes, and so promote settlement under the reclamation act. Indeed, they are essential to the welfare of every one of the great interests of the West. Forest reserves are created for two principal purposes. The first is to preserve the water supply. This is their most important use. The principal users of the water thus preserved are irrigation ranchers and settlers, cities and towns to whom their municipal water supplies are of the very first importance, users and furnishers of water power, and the users of water for domestic, manufacturing, mining, and other purposes. All these are directly dependent upon the forest reserves.

The second reason for which forest reserves are created is to preserve the timber supply for various classes of wood users. Among the more important of these are settlers under the reclamation act and other acts, for whom a cheap and accessible supply of timber for domestic uses is absolutely necessary; miners and prospectors, who are in serious danger of losing their timber supply by fire or through export by lumber companies when timber lands adjacent to their mines pass into private ownership; lumbermen, transportation companies, builders, and commercial interests in general. Although the wisdom of creating forest reserves is nearly everywhere heartily recognized, yet in a few localities there has been misunderstanding and complaint. The following statement is therefore desirable:

The forest reserve policy can be successful only when it has the full support of the people of the West. It can not safely, and should not in any case, be imposed upon them against their will. But neither can we accept the views of those whose only interest in the forest is temporary; who are anxious to reap what they have not sown and then move away, leaving desolation behind them. On the contrary, it is everywhere and always the interest of the permanent settler and the permanent business man, the man with a stake in the country, which must be considered and which must decide. The making of forest reserves within railroad and wagon-road land-grant limits will hereafter, as for the past three years, be so managed as to prevent the issue, under the act of June 4, 1897, of base for exchange or lieu selection (usually called scrip). In all cases where forest reserves within areas covered by land grants appear to be essential to the prosperity of settlers, miners, or others, the Government lands within such proposed forest reserves will, as in the recent past, be withdrawn from sale or entry pending the completion of such negotiations with the owners of the land grants as will prevent the creation of so-called scrip. It was formerly the custom to make forest reserves without first getting definite and detailed information as to the character of land and timber within their boundaries. This method of action often resulted in badly chosen boundaries and consequent injustice to settlers and others. Therefore this Administration adopted the present method of first withdrawing the land from disposal, followed by careful examination on the ground and the preparation of detailed maps and descriptions, before any forest reserve is created.

I have repeatedly called attention to the confusion which exists in Government forest matters because the work is scattered among three independent organizations. The United States is the only one of the great nations in which the forest work of the Government is not concentrated under one department, in consonance with the plainest dictates of good administration and common sense. The present arrangement is bad from every point of view. Merely to mention it is to prove that it should be terminated at once. As I have repeatedly recommended, all the forest work of the Government should be concentrated in the Department of Agriculture, where the larger part of that work is already done, where practically all of the trained foresters of the Government are employed, where chiefly in Washington there is comprehensive first-class knowledge of the problems of the reserves acquired on the ground, where all problems relating to growth from the soil are already gathered, and where all the sciences auxiliary to forestry are at hand for prompt and effective co-operation. These reasons are decisive in themselves, but it should be added that the great organizations of citizens whose interests are affected by the forest-reserves, such as the National Live Stock Association, the National Wool Growers' Association, the American Mining Congress, the national Irrigation Congress, and the National Board of Trade, have uniformly, emphatically, and most of them repeatedly, expressed themselves in favor of placing all Government forest work in the Department of Agriculture because of the peculiar adaptation of that Department for it. It is true, also, that the forest services of nearly all the great nations of the world are under the respective departments of agriculture, while in but two of the smaller nations and in one colony are they under the department of the interior. This is the result of long and varied experience and it agrees fully with the requirements of good administration in our own case.

The creation of a forest service in the Department of Agriculture will have for its important results:

First. A better handling of all forest work; because it will be under a single head, and because the vast and indispensable experience of the Department in all matters pertaining to the forest reserves, to forestry in general, and to other forms of production from the soil, will be easily and rapidly accessible.

Second. The reserves themselves, being handled from the point of view of the man in the field, instead of the man in the office, will be more easily and more widely useful to the people of the West than has been the case hitherto.

Third. Within a comparatively short time the reserves will become self-supporting. This is important, because continually and rapidly increasing appropriations will be necessary for the proper care of this exceedingly important interest of the Nation, and they can and should he offset by returns from the National forests. Under similar circumstances the forest possessions of other great nations form an important source of revenue to their governments.

Every administrative officer concerned is convinced of the necessity for the proposed consolidation of forest work in the Department of Agriculture, and I myself have urged it more than once in former messages. Again I commend it to the early and favorable consideration of the Congress. The interests of the Nation at large and of the West in particular have suffered greatly because of the delay.

I call the attention of the Congress again to the report and recommendation of the Commission on the Public Lands forwarded by me to the second session of the present Congress. The Commission has prosecuted its investigations actively during the past season, and a second report is now in an advanced stage of preparation. In connection with the work of the forest reserves I desire again to urge upon the Congress the importance of authorizing the President to set aside certain portions of these reserves or other public lands as game refuges for the preservation of the bison, the wapiti, and other large beasts once so abundant in our woods and mountains and on our great plains, and now tending toward extinction. Every support should be given to the authorities of the Yellowstone Park in their successful efforts at preserving the large creatures therein; and at very little expense portions of the public domain in other regions which are wholly unsuited to agricultural settlement could be similarly utilized. We owe it to future generations to keep alive the noble and beautiful creatures which by their presence add such distinctive character to the American wilderness. The limits of the Yellowstone Park should be extended southwards. The Canyon of the Colorado should be made a national park; and the national-park system should include the Yosemite and as many as possible of the groves of giant trees in California. The veterans of the Civil War have a claim upon the Nation such as no other body of our citizens possess. The Pension Bureau has never in its history been managed in a more satisfactory manner than is now the case.

Fifth Annual Message to Congress

December 5, 1905

Once again I call your attention to the condition of the public land laws. Recent developments have given new urgency to the need for such changes as will fit these laws to actual present conditions. The honest disposal and right use of the remaining public lands is of fundamental importance. The iniquitous methods by which the monopolizing of the public lands is being brought about under the present laws are becoming more generally known, but the existing laws do not furnish effective remedies. The recommendations of the Public Lands Commission, upon this subject are wise and should be given effect.

The creation of small irrigated farms under the Reclamation act is a powerful offset to the tendency of certain other laws to foster or permit monopoly of the land. Under that act the construction of great irrigation works has been proceeding rapidly and successfully, the lands reclaimed are eagerly taken up, and the prospect that the policy of National irrigation will accomplish all that was expected of it is bright. The act should be extended to include the State of Texas.

The Reclamation act derives much of its value from the fact that it tends to secure the greatest possible number of homes on the land, and to create communities of freeholders, in part by settlement on public lands, in part by forcing the subdivision of large private holdings before they can get water from Government irrigation works. The law requires that no right to the use of water for land in private ownership shall be sold for a tract exceeding 160 acres to any one land owner. This provision has excited active and powerful hostility, but the success of the law itself depends on the wise and firm enforcement of it.

We cannot afford to substitute tenants for freeholders on the public domain. The greater part of the remaining public lands can not be irrigated. They are at present and will probably always be of greater value for grazing than for any other purpose. This fact has led to the grazing homestead of 640 acres in Nebraska and to the proposed extension of it to other States. It is argued that a family can not be supported on 160 acres of arid grazing land. This is obviously true, but neither can a family be supported on 640 acres of much of the land to which it is proposed to apply the grazing homestead. To establish universally any such arbitrary limit would be unwise at the present time. It would probably result on the one hand in enlarging the holdings Of some of the great land owners, and on the other in needless suffering and failure on the part of a very considerable proportion of the bona fide settlers who give faith to the implied assurance of the Government that such an area is sufficient. The best use of the public grazing lands requires the careful examination and classification of these lands in order to give each settler land enough to support his family and no more. While this work is being done, and until the lands are settled, the Government should take control of the open range, under reasonable regulations suited to local needs, following the general policy--already in successful operation on the forest reserves. It is probable that the present grazing value of the open public range is scarcely more than half what it once was or what it might easily be again under careful regulation.

The forest policy of the Administration appears to enjoy the unbroken support of the people. The great users of timber are themselves forwarding the movement for forest preservation. All organized opposition to the forest preserves in the West has disappeared. Since the consolidation of all Government forest work in the National Forest Service there has been a rapid and notable gain in the usefulness of the forest reserves to the people and in public appreciation of their value. The National parks within or adjacent to forest reserves should be transferred to the charge of the Forest Service also.

The National Government already does something in connection with the construction and maintenance of the great system of levees along the lower course of the Mississippi; in my judgment it should do much more.

* * *

The law forbidding the emission of dense black or gray smoke in the city of Washington has been sustained by the courts. Something has been accomplished under it, but much remains to be done if we would preserve the capital city from defacement by the smoke nuisance. Repeated prosecutions under the law have not had the desired effect. I recommend that it be made more stringent by increasing both the minimum and maximum fine; by providing for imprisonment in cases of repeated violation, and by affording the remedy of injunction against the continuation of the operation of plants which are persistent offenders. I recommend, also, an increase in the number of inspectors, whose duty it shall be to detect violations of the act.

I call your attention to the generous act of the State of California in conferring upon the United States Government the ownership of the Yosemite Valley and the Mariposa Big Tree Grove. There should be no delay in accepting the gift, and appropriations should be made for the including thereof in the Yosemite National Park, and for the care and policing of the park. California has acted most wisely, as well as with great magnanimity, in the matter. There are certain mighty natural features of our land which should be preserved in Perpetuity for our children and our children's children. In my judgment, the Grand Canyon of the Colorado should be made into a National park. It is greatly to be wished that the State of New York should copy as regards Niagara what the

State of California has done as regards the Yosemite. Nothing should be allowed to interfere with the preservation of Niagara Falls in all their beauty and majesty. If the State cannot see to this, then it is earnestly to be wished that she should be willing to turn it over to the National Government, which should in such case (if possible, in conjunction with the Canadian Government) assume the burden and responsibility of preserving unharmed Niagara Falls; just as it should gladly assume a similar burden and responsibility for the Yosemite National Park, and as it has already assumed them for the Yellowstone National Park. Adequate provision should be made by the Congress for the proper care and supervision of all these National parks. The boundaries of the Yellowstone National Park should be extended to the south and east, to take in such portions of the abutting forest reservations as will enable the Government to protect the elk on their Winter range.

The most characteristic animal of the Western plains was the great, shaggy-maned wild ox, the bison, commonly known as buffalo. Small fragments of herds exist in a domesticated state here and there, a few of them in the Yellowstone Park. Such a herd as that on the Flathead Reservation should not be allowed to go out of existence. Either on some reservation or on some forest reserve like the Wichita reserve and game refuge provision should be made for the preservation of such a herd. I believe that the scheme would be of economic advantage, for the robe of the buffalo is of high market value, and the same is true of the robe of the crossbred animals.

Sixth Annual Message to Congress

December 3, 1906

Much is now being done for the States of the Rocky Mountains and Great Plains thru the development of the national policy of irrigation and forest preservation; no Government policy for the betterment of our internal conditions has been more fruitful of good than this. The forests of the White Mountains and Southern Appalachian regions should also be preserved; and they cannot unless the people of the States in which they lie, thru their representatives in the Congress, secure vigorous action by the National Government.

*   *   *

The destruction of the Pribilof Islands fur seals by pelagic sealing still continues. The herd which, according to the surveys made in 1874 by direction of the Congress, numbered 4,700,000, and which, according to the survey of both American and Canadian commissioners in 1891, amounted to 1,000,000, has now been reduced to about 180,000. This result has been brought about by Canadian and some other sealing vessels killing the female seals while in the water during their annual pilgrimage to and from the south, or in search of food. As a rule the female seal when killed is pregnant, and also has an unweaned pup on land, so that, for each skin taken by pelagic sealing, as a rule, three lives are destroyed--the mother, the unborn offspring, and the nursing pup, which is left to starve to death. No damage whatever is done to the herd by the carefully regulated killing on land; the custom of pelagic sealing is solely responsible for all of the present evil, and is alike indefensible from the economic standpoint and from the standpoint of humanity.

In 1896 over 16,000 young seals were found dead from starvation on the Pribilof Islands. In 1897 it was estimated that since pelagic sealing began upward of 400,000 adult female seals had been killed at sea, and over 300,000 young seals had died of starvation as the result. The revolting barbarity of such a practise, as well as the wasteful destruction which it involves, needs no demonstration and is its own condemnation. The Bering Sea Tribunal, which sat in Paris in 1893, and which decided against the claims of the United States to exclusive jurisdiction in the waters of Bering Sea and to a property right in the fur seals when outside of the three-mile limit, determined also upon certain regulations which the Tribunal considered sufficient for the proper protection and preservation of the fur seal. in, or habitually resorting to, the Bering Sea. The Tribunal by its regulations established a close season, from the 1st of May to the 31st of July, and excluded all killing in the waters within 60 miles around the Pribilof Islands. They also provided that the regulations which they had determined upon, with a view to the protection and preservation of the seals, should be submitted every five years to new examination, so as to enable both interested Governments to consider whether, in the light of past experience, there was occasion for any modification thereof.

The regulations have proved plainly inadequate to accomplish the object of protection and preservation of the fur seals, and for a long time this Government has been trying in vain to secure from Great Britain such revision and modification of the regulations as were contemplated and provided for by the award of the Tribunal of Paris. The process of destruction has been accelerated during recent years by the appearance of a number of Japanese vessels engaged in pelagic sealing. As these vessels have not been bound even by the inadequate limitations prescribed by the Tribunal of Paris, they have paid no attention either to the close season or to the sixty-mile limit imposed upon the Canadians, and have prosecuted their work up to the very islands themselves. On July 16 and 17 the crews from several Japanese vessels made raids upon the island of St. Paul, and before they were beaten off by the very meager and insufficiently armed guard, they succeeded in killing several hundred seals and carrying off the skins of most of them. Nearly all the seals killed were females and the work was done with frightful barbarity. Many of the seals appear to have been skinned alive and many were found half skinned and still alive. The raids were repelled only by the use of firearms, and five of the raiders were killed, two were wounded, and twelve captured, including the two wounded. Those captured have since been tried and sentenced to imprisonment. An attack of this kind had been wholly unlookt for, but such provision of vessels, arms, and ammunition will now be made that its repetition will not be found profitable.

Suitable representations regarding the incident have been made to the Government of Japan, and we are assured that all practicable measures will be taken by that country to prevent any recurrence of the outrage. On our part, the guard on the island will be increased and better equipped and organized, and a better revenue-cutter patrol service about the islands will be established; next season a United States war vessel will also be sent there. We have not relaxed our efforts to secure an agreement with Great Britain for adequate protection of the seal herd, and negotiations with Japan for the same purpose are in progress. The laws for the protection of the seals within the jurisdiction of the United States need revision and amendment. Only the islands of St. Paul and St. George are now, in terms, included in the Government reservation, and the other islands are also to be included. The landing of aliens as well as citizens upon the islands, without a permit from the Department of Commerce and Labor, for any purpose except in case of stress of weather or for water, should be prohibited under adequate penalties. The approach of vessels for the excepted purposes should be regulated. The authority of the Government agents on the islands should be enlarged, and the chief agent should have the powers of a committing magistrate. The entrance of a vessel into the territorial waters surrounding the islands with intent to take seals should be made a criminal offense and cause of forfeiture. Authority for seizures in such cases should be given and the presence on any such vessel of seals or sealskins, or the paraphernalia for taking them, should be made prima facie evidence of such intent. I recommend what legislation is needed to accomplish these ends; and I commend to your attention the report of Mr. Sims, of the Department of Commerce and Labor, on this subject.

In case we are compelled to abandon the hope of making arrangements with other governments to put an end to the hideous cruelty now incident to pelagic sealing, it will be a question for your serious consideration how far we should continue to protect and maintain the seal herd on land with the result of continuing such a practise, and whether it is not better to end the practice by exterminating the herd ourselves in the most humane way possible.

Special Message to Congress

December 17, 1906

The developments of the past year emphasize with increasing force the need of vigorous and immediate action to recast the public land laws and adapt them to the actual situation. The timber and stone act has demonstrated conclusively that its effect is to turn over the public timber lands to great corporations. It has done enormous harm, it is no longer needed, and it should be repealed.

The desert land act results so frequently in fraud and so comparatively seldom in making homes on land that it demands radical amendment. That provision which permits assignment before patent should be repealed, and the everyman should be required to live for not less than two years at home on the land before patent issues. Otherwise the desert land law will continue to assist speculators and other large holders to get control of land and water on the public domain by indefensible means. The commutation clause of the homestead act, in a majority of cases, defeats the purpose of the homestead act itself, which is to facilitate settlement and create homes. In theory the commutation clause should assist the honest settler and doubtless in some cases it does so. Far more often it supplies the means by which speculators and loan and mortgage companies secure possession of the land. Actual – not constructive – living at home on the land for three years should be required before commutation, unless it should appear wiser to repeal the commutation clause altogether. These matters are more fully discussed in the report of the public lands commission, to which I call your attention.

I am gravely concerned at the extremely unsatisfactory condition of the public land laws and at the prevalence of fraud under their present provisions. For much of this fraud the present laws are chiefly responsible. There is but one way by which the fraudulent acquisition of these lands can be definitely stopped, and therefore I have directed the Secretary of the Interior to allow no patent to be issued to public land under any law until by examination on the ground actual compliance with the law has been found to exist. For this purpose an increase of special agents in the general land office is urgently required. Unless it is given, bona fide would-be settlers will be put to grave inconvenience, or else the fraud will in large part go on. Further, the Secretary of the Interior should be enabled to employ enough mining experts to examine the validity of all mineral land claims, and to undertake the supervision and control of the mineral fuels still belonging to the United States. The present coal law limiting the individual entry to 160 acres puts a premium on fraud by making it impossible to develop certain types of coal fields and yet comply with the law. It is a scandal to maintain laws which sound well, but which make fraud the key without which great natural resources must remain closed. The law should give individuals and corporations, under proper government regulation and control (the details of which I shall not at present discuss) the right to work bodies of coal land large enough for profitable development. My own belief is that there should be provision for leasing coal, oil and gas rights under proper restrictions. If the additional force of special agents and mining experts I recommend is provided and well used, the result will be not only to stop the land frauds, but to prevent delays in patenting valid land claims, and to conserve the indispensable fuel resources of the nation.

Many of the existing laws affecting rights of way and privileges on public lands and reservations are illogical and unfair. Some work injustice by granting valuable rights in perpetuity without return. Others fail to protect the grantee in his possession of permanent improvements made at large expense. In fairness to the government, to the holders of rights and privileges on the public lands, and to the people whom the latter serve, I urge the revision and re-enactment of these laws in one comprehensive act, providing that the regulations and the charge now in force in many cases may be extended to all, to the end that unregulated or monopolistic control of great natural resources may not be acquired or misused for private ends.

The boundaries of the national forest reserves unavoidably include certain valuable timber lands not owned by the government. Important among them are the land grants of various railroads. For more than two years negotiations with the land grant railroads have been in progress looking toward an arrangement by which the forest on railroad lands within national forest reserves may be preserved by the removal of the present crop of timber under rules prescribed by the forest service, and its perpetuation may be assured by the transfer of the land to the government without cost. The advantage to the railroads is found in the proposal to allow them to consolidate their holdings of timber within forest reserves by exchange after deeding their lands to the government, and thus to cut within a limited time solid bodies of timber instead of alternate sections, although the amount of timber in each case would be the same. It is possible that legislation will be required to authorize this or a similar arrangement with the railroads and other owners. If so, I recommend that it be enacted.

The money value of the national forests now reserved for the use and benefit of the people exceeds considerably the sum of one thousand millions of dollars. The stumpage value of the standing timber approaches seven hundred million dollars, and, together with the range and timber lands, the water for irrigation and power, and the subsidiary values, reaches an amount equal to that of the national property now under the immediate control of the army and navy together. But this vast domain is withheld from serving the nation as freely and fully as it might by the lack of capital to develop it. The yearly running expenses are sufficiently met by the annual appropriation and the proceeds of the forests. Under the care of the forest service the latter are increasing at the rate of more than half a million dollars a year; the estimate of the appropriation for the present year is less than for last year, and it is confidently expected that by 1910 the forest service will be entirely self-supporting. In the meantime there is the most urgent need for trails, fences, cabins for the rangers, bridges, telephone lines and other items of equipment, without which the reserves cannot be handled to advantage, cannot be protected properly and cannot contribute as they should to the general welfare. Expenditures for such permanent improvements are properly chargeable to capital account. The lack of reasonable working equipment weakens the protection of the national forests and greatly limits their production. This want cannot be supplied from the appropriation for running expenses. The need is urgent. Accordingly, I recommend that the secretary of the Treasury be authorized to advance to the forest service, upon the security of standing timber, an amount, say $5,000,000, sufficient to provide a reasonable working capital for the national forests, to bear interest and to be repaid in annual installments beginning in ten years.

The national parks of the west are forested and they lie without exception within or adjacent to national forest reserves. Two years ago the latter were transferred to the care of the Secretary of Agriculture, with the satisfactory results. The same reasons which led to this transfer make advisable a similar transfer of the national parks, now in Charge of the Secretary of the Interior, and I recommend legislation to that end....

Seventh Annual Message to Congress

December 3, 1907

Irrigation should be far more extensively developed than at present, not only in the States of the Great Plains and the Rocky Mountains, but in many others, as, for instance, in large portions of the South Atlantic and Gulf States, where it should go hand in hand with the reclamation of swamp land. The Federal Government should seriously devote itself to this task, realizing that utilization of waterways and water-power, forestry, irrigation, and the reclamation of lands threatened with overflow, are all interdependent parts of the same problem. The work of the Reclamation Service in developing the larger opportunities of the western half of our country for irrigation is more important than almost any other movement. The constant purpose of the Government in connection with the Reclamation Service has been to use the water resources of the public lands for the ultimate greatest good of the greatest number; in other words, to put upon the land permanent home-makers, to use and develop it for themselves and for their children and children's children. There has been, of course, opposition to this work; opposition from some interested men who desire to exhaust the land for their own immediate profit without regard to the welfare of the next generation, and opposition from honest and well-meaning men who did not fully understand the subject or who did not look far enough ahead. This opposition is, I think, dying away, and our people are understanding that it would be utterly wrong to allow a few individuals to exhaust for their own temporary personal profit the resources which ought to be developed through use so as to be conserved for the permanent common advantage of the people as a whole. The effort of the Government to deal with the public land has been based upon the same principle as that of the Reclamation Service. The land law system which was designed to meet the needs of the fertile and well-watered regions of the Middle West has largely broken down when applied to the dryer regions of the Great Plains, the mountains, and much of the Pacific slope, where a farm of 160 acres is inadequate for self-support. In these regions the system lent itself to fraud, and much land passed out of the hands of the Government without passing into the hands of the home-maker. The Department of the Interior and the Department of Justice joined in prosecuting the offenders against the law; and they have accomplished much, while where the administration of the law has been defective it has been changed. But the laws themselves are defective. Three years ago a public lands commission was appointed to scrutinize the law, and defects, and recommend a remedy. Their examination specifically showed the existence of great fraud upon the public domain, and their recommendations for changes in the law were made with the design of conserving the natural resources of every part of the public lands by putting it to its best use. Especial attention was called to the prevention of settlement by the passage of great areas of public land into the hands of a few men, and to the enormous waste caused by unrestricted grazing upon the open range. The recommendations of the Public Lands Commission are sound, for they are especially in the interest of the actual homemaker; and where the small home-maker can not at present utilize the land they provide that the Government shall keep control of it so that it may not be monopolized by a few men. The Congress has not yet acted upon these recommendations; but they are so just and proper, so essential to our National welfare, that I feel confident, if the Congress will take time to consider them, that they will ultimately be adopted.

Some such legislation as that proposed is essential in order to preserve the great stretches of public grazing land which are unfit for cultivation under present methods and are valuable only for the forage which they supply. These stretches amount in all to some 300,000,000 acres, and are open to the free grazing of cattle, sheep, horses and goats, without restriction. Such a system, or lack of system, means that the range is not so much used as wasted by abuse. As the West settles the range becomes more and more over-grazed. Much of it can not be used to advantage unless it is fenced, for fencing is the only way by which to keep in check the owners of nomad flocks which roam hither and thither, utterly destroying the pastures and leaving a waste behind so that their presence is incompatible with the presence of home-makers. The existing fences are all illegal. Some of them represent the improper exclusion of actual settlers, actual home-makers, from territory which is usurped by great cattle companies. Some of them represent what is in itself a proper effort to use the range for those upon the land, and to prevent its use by nomadic outsiders. All these fences, those that are hurtful and those that are beneficial, are alike illegal and must come down. But it is an outrage that the law should necessitate such action on the part of the Administration. The unlawful fencing of public lands for private grazing must be stopped, but the necessity which occasioned it must be provided for. The Federal Government should have control of the range, whether by permit or lease, as local necessities may determine. Such control could secure the great benefit of legitimate fencing, while at the same time securing and promoting the settlement of the country. In some places it may be that the tracts of range adjacent to the homesteads of actual settlers should be allotted to them severally or in common for the summer grazing of their stock. Elsewhere it may be that a lease system would serve the purpose; the leases to be temporary and subject to the rights of settlement, and the amount charged being large enough merely to permit of the efficient and beneficial control of the range by the Government, and of the payment to the county of the equivalent of what it would otherwise receive in taxes. The destruction of the public range will continue until some such laws as these are enacted. Fully to prevent the fraud in the public lands which, through the joint action of the Interior Department and the Department of Justice, we have been endeavoring to prevent, there must be further legislation, and especially a sufficient appropriation to permit the Department of the Interior to examine certain classes of entries on the ground before they pass into private ownership. The Government should part with its title only to the actual home-maker, not to the profit-maker who does not care to make a home. Our prime object is to secure the rights and guard the interests of the small ranchman, the man who plows and pitches hay for himself. It is this small ranchman, this actual settler and homemaker, who in the long run is most hurt by permitting thefts of the public land in whatever form.

Optimism is a good characteristic, but if carried to an excess it becomes foolishness. We are prone to speak of the resources of this country as inexhaustible; this is not so. The mineral wealth of the country, the coal, iron, oil, gas, and the like, does not reproduce itself, and therefore is certain to be exhausted ultimately; and wastefulness in dealing with it to-day means that our descendants will feel the exhaustion a generation or two before they otherwise would. But there are certain other forms of waste which could be entirely stopped--the waste of soil by washing, for instance, which is among the most dangerous of all wastes now in progress in the United States, is easily preventable, so that this present enormous loss of fertility is entirely unnecessary. The preservation or replacement of the forests is one of the most important means of preventing this loss. We have made a beginning in forest preservation, but it is only a beginning. At present lumbering is the fourth greatest industry in the United States; and yet, so rapid has been the rate of exhaustion of timber in the United States in the past, and so rapidly is the remainder being exhausted, that the country is unquestionably on the verge of a timber famine which will be felt in every household in the land. There has already been a rise in the price of lumber, but there is certain to be a more rapid and heavier rise in the future. The present annual consumption of lumber is certainly three times as great as the annual growth; and if the consumption and growth continue unchanged, practically all our lumber will be exhausted in another generation, while long before the limit to complete exhaustion is reached the growing scarcity will make itself felt in many blighting ways upon our National welfare. About 20 per cent of our forested territory is now reserved in National forests; but these do not include the most valuable timber lauds, and in any event the proportion is too small to expect that the reserves can accomplish more than a mitigation of the trouble which is ahead for the nation. Far more drastic action is needed. Forests can be lumbered so as to give to the public the full use of their mercantile timber without the slightest detriment to the forest, any more than it is a detriment to a farm to furnish a harvest; so that there is no parallel between forests and mines, which can only be completely used by exhaustion. But forests, if used as all our forests have been used in the past and as most of them are still used, will be either wholly destroyed, or so damaged that many decades have to pass before effective use can be made of them again. All these facts are so obvious that it is extraordinary that it should be necessary to repeat them. Every business man in the land, every writer in the newspapers, every man or woman of an ordinary school education, ought to be able to see that immense quantities of timber are used in the country, that the forests which supply this timber are rapidly being exhausted, and that, if no change takes place, exhaustion will come comparatively soon, and that the effects of it will be felt severely in the every-day life of our people. Surely, when these facts are so obvious, there should be no delay in taking preventive measures. Yet we seem as a nation to be willing to proceed in this matter with happy-go-lucky indifference even to the immediate future. It is this attitude which permits the self-interest of a very few persons to weigh for more than the ultimate interest of all our people. There are persons who find it to their immense pecuniary benefit to destroy the forests by lumbering. They are to be blamed for thus sacrificing the future of the Nation as a whole to their own self-interest of the moment; but heavier blame attaches to the people at large for permitting such action, whether in the White Mountains, in the southern Alleghenies, or in the Rockies and Sierras. A big lumbering company, impatient for immediate returns and not caring to look far enough ahead, will often deliberately destroy all the good timber in a region, hoping afterwards to move on to some new country. The shiftless man of small means, who does not care to become an actual home-maker but would like immediate profit, will find it to his advantage to take up timber land simply to turn it over to such a big company, and leave it valueless for future settlers. A big mine owner, anxious only to develop his mine at the moment, will care only to cut all the timber that he wishes without regard to the future-- probably net looking ahead to the condition of the country when the forests are exhausted, any more than he does to the condition when the mine is worked out. I do not blame these men nearly as much as I blame the supine public opinion, the indifferent public opinion, which permits their action to go unchecked. Of course to check the waste of timber means that there must be on the part of the public the acceptance of a temporary restriction in the lavish use of the timber, in order to prevent the total loss of this use in the future. There are plenty of men in public and private life who actually advocate the continuance of the present system of unchecked and wasteful extravagance, using as an argument the fact that to check it will of course mean interference with the ease and comfort of certain people who now get lumber at less cost than they ought to pay, at the expense of the future generations. Some of these persons actually demand that the present forest reserves be thrown open to destruction, because, forsooth, they think that thereby the price of lumber could be put down again for two or three or more years. Their attitude is precisely like that of an agitator protesting against the outlay of money by farmers on manure and in taking care of their farms generally. Undoubtedly, if the average farmer were content absolutely to ruin his farm, he could for two or three years avoid spending any money on it,

PROCEEDINGS OF A CONFEREFCE OF GOVERNORS OPENING ADDRESS BY THE PRESIDENT

May 13, 1908

Governors of the several States; and Gentlemen:

I welcome you to this Conference at the White House. You have come hither at my request, so that we may join together to consider the question of the conservation and use of the great fundamental sources of wealth of this Nation.

So vital is this question, that for the first time in our history the chief executive officers of the States separately, and of the States together forming the Nation, have met to consider it. It is the chief material question that confronts us, second only--and second always--to the great fundamental questions of morality.

With the governors come men from each State chosen for their special acquaintance with the terms of the problem that is before us. Among them are experts in natural resources and representatives of national organizations concerned in the development and use of these resources; the Senators and Representatives in Congress; the Supreme Court, the Cabinet, and the Inland Waterways Commission have likewise been invited to the Conference, which is therefore national in a peculiar sense.

This Conference on the conservation of natural resources is in effect a meeting of the representatives of all the people of the United States called to consider the weightiest problem now before the Nation; and the occasion for the meeting lies in the fact that the natural resources of our country are in danger of exhaustion if we permit the old wasteful methods of exploiting them longer to continue.

With the rise of peoples from savagery to civilization, and with the consequent growth in the extent and variety of the needs of the average man, there comes a steadily increasing growth of the amount demanded by this average man from the actual resources of the country. And yet, rather curiously, at the same time that there comes that increase in what the average man demands from the resources, he is apt to grow to lose the sense of his dependence upon nature. He lives in big cities. He deals in industries that do not bring him in close touch with nature. He does not realize the demands he is making upon nature. For instance, he finds, as he has found before in many parts of this country, that it is cheaper to build his house of concrete than of wood, learning in this way only that he has allowed the woods to become exhausted. That is happening, as you know, in parts of this country at this very time.

Savages, and very primitive peoples generally, concern themselves only with superficial natural resources; with those which they obtain from the actual surface of the ground. As peoples become a little less primitive, their industries, although in a rude manner, are extended to resources below the surface; then, with what we call civilization and the extension of knowledge, more resources come into use, industries are multiplied, and foresight begins to become a necessary and prominent factor in life. Crops are cultivated; animals are domesticated; and metals are mastered.

We can not do any of these things without foresight, and we can not, when the nation becomes fully civilized and very rich, continue to be civilized and rich unless the nation shows more foresight than we are showing at this moment as a nation.

Every step of the progress of mankind is marked by the discovery and use of natural resources previously unused. Without such progressive knowledge and utilization of natural resources population could not grow, nor industries multiply, nor the hidden wealth of the earth be developed for the benefit of mankind.

From the first beginnings of civilization, on the banks of the Nile and the Euphrates, the industrial progress of the world has gone on slowly, with occasional set-backs, but on the whole steadily, through tens of centuries to the present day.

It never does advance by jumps, gentlemen. It always goes slowly. There are occasional set-backs, but on the whole it goes steadily.

But of late the rapidity of the process has increased at such a rate that more space has been actually covered during the century and a quarter occupied by our national life than during the preceding six thousand years that take us back to the earliest monuments of Egypt, to the earliest cities of the Babylonian plain.

Now, I ask you to think what that means; and I am speaking with historic literalness. In the development, the use, and therefore the exhaustion of certain of the natural resources, the progress has been more rapid in the past century and a quarter than during all preceding time of which we have record.

When the founders of this nation met at Independence Hall in Philadelphia the conditions of commerce had not fundamentally changed from what they were when the Phoenician keels first furrowed the lonely waters of the Mediterranean.

You turn to Homer--some of you did in your school days, even if you do not now --and you will see that he spoke, not of the Mediterranean but of one corner of the Egean only, as a limitless waste of water which no one had traversed. There is now no nook of the earth that we are not searching.

When our forefathers met in Independence Hall, the differences were those of degrees, not of kind, and they were not in all cases even those of degree. Mining was carried on fundamentally as it had been carried on by the Pharaohs in the countries adjacent to the Red Sea. Explorers now-a-days by the shores of the Red Sea strike countries that they call new, but they find in them mines, with sculptures of the Pharaohs, showing that those mines were worked out and exhausted thousands of years before the Christian era.

In 1776 the wares of the merchants of Boston, of Charleston, like the wares of the merchants of Nineveh and Sidon, if they went by water, were carried by boats propelled by sails or oars; if they went by land were carried in wagons drawn by beasts of draft or in packs on the backs of beasts of burden. The ships that crossed the high seas were better than the ships that three thousand years before crossed the Egean, but they were of the same type, after all--they were wooden ships propelled by sails. There the difference was one of degree in our favor. On shore the difference was one of degree against us, for on land the roads, at the end of the eighteenth century, when this country became a nation, were not as good as the roads of the Roman Empire, while the service of the posts, at any rate prior to the days of Benjamin Franklin, was probably inferior. In the previous eighteen hundred years there had been a retrogression in roads and in postal service.

In Washington's time anthracite coal was known only as a useless black stone; and the great fields of bituminous coal were undiscovered. As steam was unknown, the use of coal for power production was undreamed of. Water was practically the only source of power, saved the labor of men and animals; and this power was used only in the most primitive fashion. But a few small iron deposits had been found in this country, and the use of iron by our countrymen was very small. Wood was practically the only fuel, and what lumber was sawed was consumed locally, while the forests were regarded chiefly as obstructions to settlement and cultivation. The man who cut down a tree was held to have conferred a service upon his fellows.

Such was the degree of progress to which civilized mankind had attained when this nation began its career. It is almost impossible for us in this day to realize how little our Revolutionary ancestors knew of the great store of natural resources whose discovery and use have been such vital factors in the growth and greatness of this Nation, and how little they required to take from this store in order to satisfy their needs.

Since then our knowledge and use of the resources of the present territory of the United States have increased a hundred-fold. Indeed, the growth of this Nation by leaps and bounds makes one of the most striking and important chapters in the history of the world. Its growth has been due to the rapid development, and alas that it should be said, to the rapid destruction, of our natural resources. Nature has supplied to us in the United States, and still supplies to us, more kinds of resources in a more lavish degree than has ever been the case at any other time or with any other people. Our position in the world has been attained by the extent and thoroughness of the control we have achieved over nature; but we are more, and not less, dependent upon what she furnishes than at any previous time of history since the days of primitive man.

Yet our fathers, though they knew so little of the resources of the country, exercised a wise forethought in reference thereto. Washington clearly saw that the perpetuity of the States could only be secured by union, and that the only feasible basis of union was an economic one; in other words, that it must be based on the development and use of their natural resources. Accordingly, he helped to outline a scheme of commercial development, and by his influence an interstate waterways commission was appointed by Virginia and Maryland.

It met near where we are now meeting, in Alexandria, adjourned to Mount Vernon, and took up the consideration of interstate commerce by the only means then available, that of water; and the trouble we have since had with the railways has been mainly due to the fact that naturally our forefathers could not divine that the iron road would become the interstate and international highway, instead of the old route by water. Further conferences were arranged, first at Annapolis, and then at Philadelphia. It was in Philadelphia that the representatives of all the States met for what was in its original conception merely a waterways conference; but when they had closed their deliberations the outcome was the Constitution which made the States into a nation.

The Constitution of the United States thus grew in large part out of the necessity for united action in the wise of one of our natural resources. The wise use of all of our natural resources, which are our national resources as well, is the great material question of today. I have asked you to come together now because the enormous consumption of these resources, and the threat of imminent exhaustion of some of them, due to reckless and wasteful use, once more calls for common effort, common action.

We want to take action that will prevent the advent of a woodless age, and defer as long as possible the advent of an ironless age.

Since the days when the Constitution was adopted, steam and electricity have revolutionized the industrial world. Nowhere has the revolution been so great as in our own country. The discovery and utilization of mineral fuels and alloys have given us the lead over all other nations in the production of steel. The discovery and utilization of coal and iron have given us our railways, and have led to such industrial development as has never before been seen. The vast wealth of lumber in our forests, the riches of our soils and mines, the discovery of gold and mineral oils, combined with the efficiency of our transportation, have made the conditions of our life unparalleled in comfort and convenience.

A great many of these things are truisms. Much of what I say is so familiar to us that it seems commonplace to repeat it; but familiar though it is, I do not think as a nation we understand what its real bearing is. It is so familiar that we disregard it.

The steadily increasing drain on these natural resources has promoted to an extraordinary degree the complexity of our industrial and social life. Moreover, this unexampled development has had a determining effect upon the character and opinions of our people. The demand for efficiency in the great task has given us vigor, effectiveness, decision, and power, and a capacity for achievement which in its own lines has never yet been matched. So great and so rapid has been our material growth that there has been a tendency to lag behind in spiritual and moral growth [laughter and applause]; but that is not the subject upon which I speak to you today.

Disregarding for the moment the question of moral purpose, it is safe to say that the prosperity of our people depends directly on the energy and intelligence with which our natural resources are used. It is equally clear that these resources are the final basis of national power and perpetuity. Finally, it is ominously evident that these resources are in ✓ the course of rapid exhaustion.

This Nation began with the belief that its landed possessions were illimitable and capable of supporting all the people who might care to make our country their home; but already the limit of unsettled land is in sight, and indeed but little land fitted for agriculture now remains unoccupied save what can be reclaimed by irrigation and drainage--a subject with which this Conference is partly to deal. We began with an unapproached heritage of forests; more than half of the timber is gone. We began with coal fields more extensive than those of any other nation and with iron ores regarded as inexhaustible, and many experts now declare that the end of both iron and coal is in sight.

The mere increase in our consumption of coal during 1907 over 1906 exceeded the total consumption in 1876, the Centennial year. This is a striking fact: Thirty years went by, and the mere surplus of use of one year over the preceding year exceeded all that was used in 1876--and we thought we were pretty busy people even then. The enormous stores of mineral oil and gas are largely gone; and those Governors who have in their States cities built up by natural gas, where the natural gas has since been exhausted, can tell us something of what that means. Our natural waterways are not gone, but they have been so injured by neglect, and by the division of responsibility and utter lack of system in dealing with them, that there is less navigation on them now than there was fifty years ago. Finally, we began with soils of unexampled fertility, and we have so impoverished them by injudicious use and by failing to check erosion that their crop-producing power is diminishing instead of increasing. In a word, we have thoughtlessly, and to a large degree unnecessarily, diminished the resources upon which not only our prosperity but the prosperity of our children and our children's children must always depend.

We have become great in a material sense because of the lavish use of our resources, and we have just reason to be proud of our growth. But the time has come to inquire seriously what will happen when our forests are gone, when the coal, the iron, the oil, and the gas are exhausted, when the soils shall have been still further impoverished and washed into the streams, polluting the rivers, denuding the fields, and obstructing navigation. These questions do not relate only to the next century or to the next generation. One distinguishing characteristic of really civilized men is foresight; we have to, as a nation, exercise foresight for this nation in the future; and if we do not exercise that foresight, dark will be the future! We should exercise foresight now, as the ordinarily prudent man exercises foresight in conserving and wisely using the property which contains the assurance of well-being for himself and his children. We want to see a man own his farm rather than rent it, because we want to see it an object to him to transfer it in better order to his children. We want to see him exercise forethought for the next generation. We need to exercise it in some fashion ourselves as a nation for the next generation.

The natural resources I have enumerated can be divided into two sharply distinguished classes accordingly as they are or are not capable of renewal. Mines if used must necessarily be exhausted. The minerals do not and can not renew themselves. Therefore in dealing with the coal, the oil, the gas, the iron, the metals generally, all that we can do is to try to see that they are wisely used. The exhaustion is certain to come in time. We can trust that it will be deferred long enough to enable the extraordinarily inventive genius of our people to devise means and methods for more or less adequately replacing what is lost; but the exhaustion is sure to come.

The second class of resources consists of those which can not only be used in such manner as to leave them undiminished for our children, but can actually be improved by wise use. The soil, the forests, the waterways come in this category. Every one knows that a really good farmer leaves his farm more valuable at the end of his life than it was when he first took hold of it. So with the waterways. So with the forests. In dealing with mineral resources, man is able to improve on nature only by putting the resources to a beneficial use which in the end exhausts them; but in dealing with the soil and its products man can improve on nature by compelling the resources to renew and even reconstruct themselves in such manner as to serve increasingly beneficial uses--while the living waters can be so controlled as to multiply their benefits.

Neither the primitive man nor the pioneer was aware of any duty to posterity in dealing with the renewable resources. When the American settler felled the forests, he felt that there was plenty of forest left for the sons who came after him. When he exhausted the soil of his farm, he felt that his son could go West and take up another. The Kentuckian or the Ohioan felled the forest and expected his son to move west and fell other forests on the banks of the Mississippi; the Georgian exhausted his farm and moved into Alabama or to the mouth of the Yazoo to take another. So it was with his immediate successors. When the soil-wash from the farmer's field choked the neighboring river, the only thought was to use the railway rather than the boats to move produce and supplies. That was so up to the generation that preceded ours.

Now all this is changed. On the average the son of the farmer of today must make his living on his father's farm. There is no difficulty in doing this if the father will exercise wisdom. No wise use of a farm exhausts its fertility. So with the forests. We are over the verge of a timber famine in this country, and it is unpardonable for the Nation or the States to permit any further cutting of our timber save in accordance with a system which will provide that the next generation shall see the timber increased instead of diminished.

Just let me interject one word as to a particular type of folly of which it ought not to be necessary to speak. We stop wasteful cutting of timber; that of course makes a slight shortage at the moment. To avoid that slight shortage at the moment, there are certain people so foolish that they will incur absolute shortage in the future, and they are willing to stop all attempts to conserve the forests, because of course by wastefully using them at the moment we can for a year or two provide against any lack of wood. That is like providing for the farmer's family to live sumptuously on the flesh of the milch cow. Any farmer can live pretty well for a year if he is content not to live at all the year after.

We can, moreover, add enormous tracts of the most valuable possible agricultural land to the national domain by irrigation in the arid and semi-arid regions, and by drainage of great tracts of swamp land in the humid regions. We can enormously increase our transportation facilities by the canalization of our rivers so as to complete a great system of waterways on the Pacific, Atlantic, and Gulf coasts and in the Mississippi Valley, from the Great Plains to the Alleghenies, and from the northern lakes to the mouth of the mighty Father of Waters. But all these various uses of our natural resources are so closely connected that they should be coordinated, and should be treated as part of one coherent plan and not in haphazard and piecemeal fashion.

It is largely because of this that I appointed the Waterways Commission last year, and that I sought to perpetuate its work. There are members of the coordinate branch present. The reason this meeting takes place is because we had that waterways commission last year. I had to prosecute the work by myself. I have asked Congress to pass a bill giving some small sum of money for the perpetuation of that Commission. If Congress does not act, I will perpetuate the Commission ✓ anyway, [Great applause] but of course it is a great deal better that Congress should act; [Applause] it enables the work to be more effectively done. I hope there will be action. But the Commission will go ahead.

I wish to take this opportunity to express in heartiest fashion my acknowledgment to all the members of the Commission. At great personal sacrifice of time and effort they have rendered a service to the public for which we can not be too grateful. Especial credit is due to the initiative, the energy, the devotion to duty, and the farsightedness of Gifford Pinchot, to whom we owe so much of the progress we have already made in handling this matter of the coordination and conservation of natural resources. If it had not been for him this convention neither would nor could have been called.

We are coming to recognize as never before the right of the Nation to guard its own future in the essential matter of natural resources. In the past we have admitted the right of the individual to injure the future of the Republic for his own present profit. In fact there has been a good deal of a demand for unrestricted individualism, for the right of the individual to injure the future of all of us for his own temporary and immediate profit. The time has come for a change. As a people we have the right and the duty, second to none other but the right and duty of obeying the moral law, of requiring and doing justice, to protect ourselves and our children against the wasteful development of our natural resources, whether that waste is caused by the actual destruction of such resources or by making them impossible of development hereafter.

Any right thinking father earnestly desires and strives to leave his son both an untarnished name and a reasonable equipment for the struggle of life. So this Nation as a whole should earnestly desire and strive to leave to the next generation the national honor unstained and the national resources unexhausted. There are signs that both the Nation and the States are waking to a realization of this great truth-

On March 10, 1908, the Supreme Court of Maine rendered an exceedingly important judicial decision. This opinion was rendered in response to questions as to the right of the Legislature to restrict the cutting of trees on private land for the prevention of droughts and floods, the preservation of the natural water supply, and the prevention of the erosion of such lands, and the consequent filling up of rivers, ponds, and lakes. The forests and water power of Maine constitute the larger part of her wealth and form the basis of her industrial life, and the question submitted by the Maine Senate to the Supreme Court and the answer of the Supreme Court alike bear testimony to the wisdom of the people of Maine, and clearly define a policy of conservation of natural resources, the adoption of which is of vital importance not merely to Maine but to the whole country.

Such a policy will preserve soil, forests, water power as a heritage for the children and the children's children of the men and women of this generation; for any enactment that provides for the wise utilization of the forests, whether in public or private ownership, and for the conservation of the water resources of the country, must necessarily be legislation that will promote both private and public welfare; for flood prevention, water-power development, preservation of the soil, and improvement of navigable rivers are all promoted by such a policy of forest conservation.

The opinion of the Maine Supreme Bench sets forth unequivocally the principle that the property rights of the individual are subordinate to the rights of the community, and especially that the waste of wild timber land derived originally from the State, involving as it would the impoverishment of the State and its People and thereby defeating a great purpose of government, may properly be prevented by State restrictions.

The Court says that there are two reasons why the right of the public to control and limit the use of private property is peculiarly applicable to property in land:

First, such property is not the result of productive labor, but is derived solely from the State itself, the original owner; second, the amount of land being incapable of increase, if the owners of large tracts can waste them at will without State restriction, the State and its people may be helplessly impoverished and one great purpose of government defeated. * * * We do not think the proposed legislation would operate to "take" private property within the inhibition of the Constitution. While it might restrict the owner of wild and uncultivated lands in his use of them, might delay his taking some of the product, might delay his anticipated profits and even thereby might cause him some loss of profit, it would nevertheless leave him his lands, their product and increase, untouched, and without diminution of title, estate, or quantity. He would still have large measure of control and large opportunity to realize values. He might suffer delay but not deprivation. * * * The proposed legislation * * * would be within the legislative power and would not operate as a taking of private property for which compensation must be made.

The Court of Errors and Appeals of New Jersey has adopted a similar view, which has recently been sustained by the Supreme Court of the United States. In delivering the opinion of the Court on April 6, 1908, Mr. Justice Holmes said:

The State as quasi sovereign and representative of the interests of the public has a standing in court to protect the atmosphere, the water, and the forests within its territory, irrespective of the assent or dissent of the private owners of the land most immediately concerned. * * * It appears to us that few public interests are more obvious, indisputable and independent of particular theory than the interest of the public of a State to maintain the rivers that are wholly within it substantially undiminished, except by such drafts upon them as the guardian of the public welfare may permit for the purpose of turning them to a more perfect use.

This public interest is omnipresent wherever there is a State, and grows more pressing as population grows.

Not as a dictum of law, which I cannot make, but as a dictum of moral, I wish to say that this applies to more than the forests and streams. The learned Justice proceeds:

We are of opinion, further, that the constitutional power of the State to insist that its natural advantages shall remain unimpaired by its citizens is not dependent upon any nice estimate of the extent of present use or speculation as to future needs. The legal conception of the necessary is apt to be confined to somewhat rudimentary wants, and there are benefits from a great river that might escape a lawyer's view.

I have simply quoted.

But the State is not required to submit even to an esthetic analysis. Any analysis may be inadequate. It finds itself in possession of what all admit to be a great public good, and want it has it may keep and give no one a reason for its will.

These decisions reach the root of the idea of conservation of our resources in the interests of our people.

Finally, let us remember that the conservation of our natural resources, though the gravest problem of today, is yet but part of another and greater problem to which this Nation is not yet awake, but to which it will awake in time, and with which it must hereafter grapple if it is to live--the problem of national efficiency, the patriotic duty of insuring the safety and continuance of the Nation. When the People of the United States consciously undertake to raise themselves as citizens, and the Nation and the States in their several spheres, to the highest pitch of excellence in private, State, and national life, and to do this because it is the first of all the duties of true patriotism, then and not till then the future of this Nation, in quality and in time, will be assured.

Eighth Annual Message to Congress

December 8, 1908

FORESTS

If there is any one duty which more than another we owe it to our children and our children's children to perform at once, it is to save the forests of this country, for they constitute the first and most important element in the conservation of the natural resources of the country. There are of course two kinds of natural resources, One is the kind which can only be used as part of a process of exhaustion; this is true of mines, natural oil and gas wells, and the like. The other, and of course ultimately by far the most important, includes the resources which can be improved in the process of wise use; the soil, the rivers, and the forests come under this head. Any really civilized nation will so use all of these three great national assets that the nation will have their benefit in the future. Just as a farmer, after all his life making his living from his farm, will, if he is an expert farmer, leave it as an asset of increased value to his son, so we should leave our national domain to our children, increased in value and not worn out. There are small sections of our own country, in the East and the West, in the Adriondacks, the White Mountains, and the Appalachians, and in the Rocky Mountains, where we can already see for ourselves the damage in the shape of permanent injury to the soil and the river systems which comes from reckless deforestation. It matters not whether this deforestation is due to the actual reckless cutting of timber, to the fires that inevitably follow such reckless cutting of timber, or to reckless and uncontrolled grazing, especially by the great migratory bands of sheep, the unchecked wandering of which over the country means destruction to forests and disaster to the small home makers, the settlers of limited means. Shortsighted persons, or persons blinded to the future by desire to make money in every way out of the present, sometimes speak as if no great damage would be done by the reckless destruction of our forests. It is difficult to have patience with the arguments of these persons. Thanks to our own recklessness in the use of our splendid forests, we have already crossed the verge of a timber famine in this country, and no measures that we now take can, at least for many years, undo the mischief that has already been done. But we can prevent further mischief being done; and it would be in the highest degree reprehensible to let any consideration of temporary convenience or temporary cost interfere with such action, especially as regards the National Forests which the nation can now, at this very moment, control.

All serious students of the question are aware of the great damage that has been done in the Mediterranean countries of Europe, Asia, and Africa by deforestation. The similar damage that has been done in Eastern Asia is less well known. A recent investigation into conditions in North China by Mr. Frank N. Meyer, of the Bureau of Plant Industry of the United States Department of Agriculture, has incidentally furnished in very striking fashion proof of the ruin that comes from reckless deforestation of mountains, and of the further fact that the damage once done may prove practically irreparable. So important are these investigations that I herewith attach as an appendix to my message certain photographs showing present conditions in China. They show in vivid fashion the appalling desolation, taking the shape of barren mountains and gravel and sand-covered plains, which immediately follows and depends upon the deforestation of the mountains. Not many centuries ago the country of northern China was one of the most fertile and beautiful spots in the entire world, and was heavily forested. We know this not only from the old Chinese records, but from the accounts given by the traveler, Marco Polo. He, for instance, mentions that in visiting the provinces of Shansi and Shensi he observed many plantations of mulberry trees. Now there is hardly a single mulberry tree in either of these provinces, and the culture of the silkworm has moved farther south, to regions of atmospheric moisture. As an illustration of the complete change in the rivers, we may take Polo's statement that a certain river, the Hun Ho, was so large and deep that merchants ascended it from the sea with heavily laden boats; today this river is simply a broad sandy bed, with shallow, rapid currents wandering hither and thither across it, absolutely unnavigable. But we do not have to depend upon written records. The dry wells, and the wells with water far below the former watermark, bear testimony to the good days of the past and the evil days of the present. Wherever the native vegetation has been allowed to remain, as, for instance, here and there around a sacred temple or imperial burying ground, there are still huge trees and tangled jungle, fragments of the glorious ancient forests. The thick, matted forest growth formerly covered the mountains to their summits. All natural factors favored this dense forest growth, and as long as it was permitted to exist the plains at the foot of the mountains were among the most fertile on the globe, and the whole country was a garden. Not the slightest effort was made, however, to prevent the unchecked cutting of the trees, or to secure reforestation. Doubtless for many centuries the tree-cutting by the inhabitants of the mountains worked but slowly in bringing about the changes that have now come to pass; doubtless for generations the inroads were scarcely noticeable. But there came a time when the forest had shrunk sufficiently to make each year's cutting a serious matter, and from that time on the destruction proceeded with appalling rapidity; for of course each year of destruction rendered the forest less able to recuperate, less able to resist next year's inroad. Mr. Meyer describes the ceaseless progress of the destruction even now, when there is so little left to destroy. Every morning men and boys go out armed with mattox or axe, scale the steepest mountain sides, and cut down and grub out, root and branch, the small trees and shrubs still to be found. The big trees disappeared centuries ago, so that now one of these is never seen save in the neighborhood of temples, where they are artificially

179

protected; and even here it takes all the watch and care of the tree-loving priests to prevent their destruction. Each family, each community, where there is no common care exercised in the interest of all of them to prevent deforestation, finds its profit in the immediate use of the fuel which would otherwise be used by some other family or some other community. In the total absence of regulation of the matter in the interest of the whole people, each small group is inevitably pushed into a policy of destruction which can not afford to take thought for the morrow. This is just one of those matters which it is fatal to leave to unsupervised individual control. The forest can only be protected by the State, by the Nation; and the liberty of action of individuals must be conditioned upon what the State or Nation determines to be necessary for the common safety.

The lesson of deforestation in China is a lesson which mankind should have learned many times already from what has occurred in other places. Denudation leaves naked soil; then gullying cuts down to the bare rock; and meanwhile the rock-waste buries the bottomlands. When the soil is gone, men must go; and the process does not take long. This ruthless destruction of the forests in northern China has brought about, or has aided in bringing about, desolation, just as the destruction of the forests in central Asia aid in bringing ruin to the once rich central Asian cities; just as the destruction of the forest in northern Africa helped towards the ruin of a region that was a fertile granary in Roman days. Shortsighted man, whether barbaric, semi-civilized, or what he mistakenly regards as fully civilized, when he has destroyed the forests, has rendered certain the ultimate destruction of the land itself. In northern China the mountains are now such as are shown by the accompanying photographs, absolutely barren peaks. Not only have the forests been destroyed, but because of their destruction the soil has been washed off the naked rock. The terrible consequence is that it is impossible now to undo the damage that has been done. Many centuries would have to pass before soil would again collect, or could be made to collect, in sufficient quantity once more to support the old-time forest growth. In consequence the Mongol Desert is practically extending eastward over northern China. The climate has changed and is still changing. It has changed even within the last half century, as the work of tree destruction has been consummated. The great masses of arboreal vegetation on the mountains formerly absorbed the heat of the sun and sent up currents of cool air which brought the moisture-laden clouds lower and forced them to precipitate in rain a part of their burden of water. Now that there is no vegetation, the barren mountains, scorched by the sun, send up currents of heated air which drive away instead of attracting the rain clouds, and cause their moisture to be disseminated. In consequence, instead of the regular and plentiful rains which existed in these regions of China when the forests were still in evidence, the unfortunate inhabitants of the deforested lands now see their crops wither for lack of rainfall, while the seasons grow more and more irregular; and as the air becomes dryer certain crops refuse longer to grow at all. That everything dries out faster than formerly is shown by the fact that the level of the wells all over the land has sunk perceptibly, many of them having become totally dry. In addition to the resulting agricultural distress, the watercourses have changed. Formerly they were narrow and deep, with an abundance of clear water the year around; for the roots and humus of the forests caught the rainwater and let it escape by slow, regular seepage. They have now become broad, shallow stream beds, in which muddy water trickles in slender currents during the dry seasons, while when it rains there are freshets, and roaring muddy torrents come tearing down, bringing disaster and destruction everywhere. Moreover, these floods and freshets, which diversify the general dryness, wash away from the mountain sides, and either wash away or cover in the valleys, the rich fertile soil which it took tens of thousands of years for Nature to form; and it is lost forever, and until the forests grow again it can not be replaced. The sand and stones from the mountain sides are washed loose and come rolling down to cover the arable lands, and in consequence, throughout this part of China, many formerly rich districts are now sandy wastes, useless for human cultivation and even for pasture. The cities have been of course seriously affected, for the streams have gradually ceased to be navigable. There is testimony that even within the memory of men now living there has been a serious diminution of the rainfall of northeastern China. The level of the Sungari River in northern Manchuria has been sensibly lowered during the last fifty years, at least partly as the result of the indiscriminate rutting of the forests forming its watershed. Almost all the rivers of northern China have become uncontrollable, and very dangerous to the dwellers along their banks, as a direct result of the destruction of the forests. The journey from Pekin to Jehol shows in melancholy fashion how the soil has been washed away from whole valleys, so that they have been converted into deserts.

In northern China this disastrous process has gone on so long and has proceeded so far that no complete remedy could be applied. There are certain mountains in China from which the soil is gone so utterly that only the slow action of the ages could again restore it; although of course much could be done to prevent the still further eastward extension of the Mongolian Desert if the Chinese Government would act at once. The accompanying cuts from photographs show the inconceivable desolation of the barren mountains in which certain of these rivers rise--mountains, be it remembered, which formerly supported dense forests of larches and firs, now unable to produce any wood, and because of their condition a source of danger to the whole country. The photographs also show the same rivers after they have passed through the mountains, the beds having become broad and sandy because of the deforestation of the mountains. One of the photographs shows a caravan passing through a valley. Formerly, when the mountains were forested, it was thickly peopled by prosperous peasants. Now the floods have carried destruction all over the land and the valley is a stony desert. Another photograph shows a mountain road covered with the stones and rocks that are brought down in the rainy season from the mountains which have already been deforested by human hands. Another shows a pebbly river-bed in southern Manchuria where what was once a great stream has dried up owing to the deforestation in the mountains. Only some scrub wood is left, which will disappear within a half century. Yet another shows the effect of one of the washouts, destroying an arable mountain side, these washouts being due to the removal of all vegetation; yet in this photograph the foreground shows that reforestation is still a possibility in places. What has thus happened in northern China, what has happened in Central Asia, in Palestine, in North Africa, in parts of the Mediterranean countries of Europe, will surely happen in our country if we do not exercise that wise forethought which should be one of the chief marks of any people calling itself civilized. Nothing should be permitted to stand in the way of the preservation of the forests, and it is criminal to permit individuals to purchase a little gain for themselves through the destruction of forests when this destruction is fatal to the well-being of the whole country in the future.

INLAND WATERWAYS

Action should be begun forthwith, during the present session of the Congress, for the improvement of our inland waterways--action which will result in giving us not only navigable but navigated rivers. We have spent hundreds of millions of dollars upon these waterways, yet the traffic on nearly all of them is steadily declining. This condition is the direct result of the absence of any comprehensive and far-seeing plan of waterway improvement, Obviously we can not continue thus to expend the revenues of the Government without return. It is poor business to spend money for inland navigation unless we get it. Inquiry into the condition of the

Mississippi and its principal tributaries reveals very many instances of the utter waste caused by the methods which have hitherto obtained for the so-called "improvement" of navigation. A striking instance is supplied by the "improvement" of the Ohio, which, begun in 1824, was continued under a single plan for half a century. In 1875 a new plan was adopted and followed for a quarter of a century. In 1902 still a different plan was adopted and has since been pursued at a rate which only promises a navigable river in from twenty to one hundred years longer. Such shortsighted, vacillating, and futile methods are accompanied by decreasing water-borne commerce and increasing traffic congestion on land, by increasing floods, and by the waste of public money. The remedy lies in abandoning the methods which have so signally failed and adopting new ones in keeping with the needs and demands of our people.

In a report on a measure introduced at the first session of the present Congress, the Secretary of War said: "The chief defect in the methods hitherto pursued lies in the absence of executive authority for originating comprehensive plans covering the country or natural divisions thereof." In this opinion I heartily concur. The present methods not only fail to give us inland navigation, but they are injurious to the army as well. What is virtually a permanent detail of the corps of engineers to civilian duty necessarily impairs the efficiency of our military establishment. The military engineers have undoubtedly done efficient work in actual construction, but they are necessarily unsuited by their training and traditions to take the broad view, and to gather and transmit to the Congress the commercial and industrial information and forecasts, upon which waterway improvement must always so largely rest. Furthermore, they have failed to grasp the great underlying fact that every stream is a unit from its source to its mouth, and that all its uses are interdependent. Prominent officers of the Engineer Corps have recently even gone so far as to assert in print that waterways are not dependent upon the conservation of the forests about their headwaters. This position is opposed to all the recent work of the scientific bureaus of the Government and to the general experience of mankind. A physician who disbelieved in vaccination would not be the right man to handle an epidemic of smallpox, nor should we leave a doctor skeptical about the transmission of yellow fever by the Stegomyia mosquito in charge of sanitation at Havana or Panama. So with the improvement of our rivers; it is no longer wise or safe to leave this great work in the hands of men who fail to grasp the essential relations between navigation and general development and to assimilate and use the central facts about our streams.

Until the work of river improvement is undertaken in a modern way it can not have results that will meet the needs of this modern nation. These needs should be met without further dilly-dallying or delay. The plan which promises the best and quickest results is that of a permanent commission authorized to coordinate the work of all the Government departments relating to waterways, and to frame and supervise the execution of a comprehensive plan. Under such a commission the actual work of construction might be entrusted to the reclamation service; or to the military engineers acting with a sufficient number of civilians to continue the work in time of war; or it might be divided between the reclamation service and the corps of engineers. Funds should be provided from current revenues if it is deemed wise--otherwise from the sale of bonds. The essential thing is that the work should go forward under the best possible plan, and with the least possible delay. We should have a new type of work and a new organization for planning and directing it. The time for playing with our waterways is past. The country demands results.

NATIONAL PARKS

I urge that all our National parks adjacent to National forests be placed completely under the control of the forest service of the Agricultural Department, instead of leaving them as they now are, under the Interior Department and policed by the army. The Congress should provide for superintendents with adequate corps of first-class civilian scouts, or rangers, and, further, place the road construction under the superintendent instead of leaving it with the War Department. Such a change in park management would result in economy and avoid the difficulties of administration which now arise from having the responsibility of care and protection divided between different departments. The need for this course is peculiarly great in the Yellowstone Park. This, like the Yosemite, is a great wonderland, and should be kept as a national playground. In both, all wild things should be protected and the scenery kept wholly unmarred. I am happy to say that I have been able to set aside in various parts of the country small, well-chosen tracts of ground to serve as sanctuaries and nurseries for wild creatures.

Special Message To the Senate and House of Representatives

January 22, 1909

I transmit herewith a report of the National Conservation Commission, together with the accompanying papers. This report, which is the outgrowth of the Conference of Governors last May, was unanimously approved by the recent joint conference held in this city between the National Conservation Commission and governors of states, state conservation commissions, and conservation committees of great organizations of citizens. It is, therefore, in a peculiar sense, representative of the whole nation and all its parts.

With the statements and conclusions of this report I heartily concur, and I commend it to the thoughtful consideration both of the Congress and of our people generally. It is one of the most fundamentally important documents ever laid before the American people. It contains the first inventory of its natural resources ever made by any nation. In condensed form it presents a statement of our available capital in material resources, which are the means of progress, and calls attention to the essential conditions upon which the perpetuity, safety, and welfare of this nation now rest and must always continue to rest. It deserves, and should have, the widest possible distribution among the people. . . .

The National Conservation Commission wisely confined its report to the statement of facts and principles, leaving the Executive to recommend the specific steps to which these facts and principles inevitably lead. Accordingly, I call your attention to some of the larger features of the situation disclosed by the report and to the action thereby clearly demanded for the general good.

WATERS

The report says:

Within recent months it has been recognized and demanded by the people, through many thousand delegates from all states assembled in convention in different sections of the country, that the waterways should and must be improved promptly and effectively as a means of maintaining national prosperity.

The first requisite for waterway improvement is the control of the waters in such manner as to reduce floods and regulate the regimen of the navigable rivers. The second requisite is development of terminals and connection in such manner as to regulate commerce.

Accordingly, I urge that the broad plan for the development of our waterways recommended by the Inland Waterways Commission be put in effect without delay. It provides for a comprehensive system of waterway improvement extending to all the uses of the waters and benefits to be derived from their control, including navigation, the development of power, the extension of irrigation, the drainage of swamp and overflow lands, the prevention of soil wash, and the purification of streams for water supply. It proposes to carry out the work by coordinating agencies in the federal departments through the medium of an administrative commission or board acting in cooperation with the states and other organizations and individual citizens.

The work of waterway development should be undertaken without delay. Meritorious projects in known conformity with the general outlines of any comprehensive plan should proceed at once. The cost of the whole work should be met by direct appropriation, if possible, but, if necessary, by the issue of bonds in small denominations.

It is especially important that the development of waterpower should be guarded with the utmost care both by the national government and by the states in order to protect the people against the upgrowth of monopoly and to insure to them a fair share in the benefits which will follow the development of this great asset which belongs to the people and should be controlled by them.

FORESTS

I urge that provision be made for both protection and more rapid development of the national forests. Otherwise, either the increasing use of these forests by the people must be checked or their protection against fire must be dangerously weakened. If we compare the actual fire damage on similar areas on private and national forest lands during the past year, the government fire patrol saved commercial timber worth as much as the total cost of caring for all national forests at the present rate for about ten years.

I especially commend to the Congress the facts presented by the commission as to the relation between forests and stream flow in its bearing upon the importance of the forest lands in national ownership. Without an understanding of this intimate relation the conservation of both these natural resources must largely fail.

189

The time has fully arrived for recognizing in the law the responsibility to the community, the state, and the nation which rests upon the private owners of private lands. The ownership of forest land is a public trust. The man who would so handle his forest as to cause erosion and to injure stream flow must be not only educated but he must be controlled.

The report of the National Conservation Commission says:

> Forests in private ownership cannot be conserved unless they are protected from fire. We need good fire laws, well-enforced. Fire control is impossible without an adequate force of men whose sole duty is fire patrol during the dangerous season.

I hold as first among the tasks before the states and the nation in their respective shares in forest conservation the organization of efficient fire patrols and the enactment of good fire laws on the part of the states.

The report says further:

> Present tax laws prevent reforestation of cut-over land and the perpetuation of existing forests by use. An annual tax upon the land itself, exclusive of the timber, and a tax upon the timber when cut is well-adapted to actual conditions of forest investment and is practicable and certain. It is far better that forest land should pay a moderate tax permanently than that it should pay an excessive revenue temporarily and then cease to yield at all.

Second only in importance to good fire laws, well-enforced, is the enactment of tax laws which will permit the perpetuation of existing forests by use.

LANDS

With our increasing population the time is not far distant when the problem of supplying our people with food will become pressing. The possible additions to our arable area are not great, and it will become necessary to obtain much larger crops from the land, as is now done in more densely settled countries. To do this, we need better farm practice and better strains of wheat, corn, and other crop plants, with a reduction in losses from soil erosion and from insects, animals, and other enemies of agriculture. The United States Department of Agriculture is doing excellent work in these directions and it should be liberally supported.

The remaining public lands should be classified and the arable lands disposed of to homemakers. In their interest the Timber and Stone Act and the commutation clause of the Homestead Act should be repealed, and the Desert-Land Law should be modified in accordance with the recommendations of the Public Lands Commission.

The use of the public grazing lands should be regulated in such ways as to improve and conserve their value.

Rights to the surface of the public land should be separated from rights to forests upon it and to minerals beneath it, and these should be subject to separate disposal.

The coal, oil, gas, and phosphate rights still remaining with the government should be withdrawn from entry and leased under conditions favorable for economic development.

MINERALS

The consumption of nearly all of our mineral products is increasing more rapidly than our population. Our mineral waste is about one-sixth of our product, or nearly $1 million for each working day in the year. The loss of structural materials through fire is about another million a day. The loss of life in the mines is appalling. The larger part of these losses of life and property can be avoided.

Our mineral resources are limited in quantity and cannot be increased or reproduced. With the rapidly increasing rate of consumption, the supply will be exhausted while yet the nation is in its infancy unless better methods are devised or substitutes are found. Further investigation is urgently needed in order to improve methods and to develop and apply substitutes.

It is of the utmost importance that a Bureau of Mines be established in accordance with the pending bill to reduce the loss of life in mines and the waste of mineral resources, and to investigate the methods and substitutes for prolonging the duration of our mineral supplies. Both the need and the public demand for such a bureau are rapidly becoming more urgent. It should cooperate with the states in supplying data to serve as a basis for state mine regulations. The establishment of this bureau will mean merely the transfer from other bureaus of work which it is agreed should be transferred and slightly enlarged and reorganized for these purposes.

CONCLUSIONS

The joint conference already mentioned adopted two resolutions to which I call your special attention. The first was intended to promote cooperation between the states and the nation upon all of the great questions here discussed. It is as follows:

> *Resolved,* that a joint committee be appointed by the chairman to consist of six members of state conservation commissions and three members of the National Conservation Commission, whose duty it shall be to prepare and present to the state and national commissions, and through them to the governors and the President, a plan for united action by all organizations concerned with the conservation of natural resources. . . .

The second resolution of the joint conference to which I refer calls upon the Congress to provide the means for such cooperation. The principle of the community of interest among all our people in the great natural resources runs through the report of the National Conservation Commission and the proceedings of the joint conference. These resources, which form the common basis of our welfare, can be wisely developed, rightly used, and prudently conserved only by the common action of all the people acting through their representatives in state and nation. Hence the fundamental necessity for cooperation. Without it we shall accomplish but little, and that little badly. The resolution follows:

> We also especially urge on the Congress of the United States the high desirability of maintaining a national commission on the conservation of the resources of the country, empowered to cooperate with state commissions to the end that every sovereign commonwealth and every section of the country may attain the high degree of prosperity and the sureness of perpetuity naturally arising in the abundant resources

and the vigor, intelligence, and patriotism of
our people.

In this recommendation I most heartily concur, and I
urge that an appropriation of at least $50,000 be made to
cover the expenses of the National Conservation
Commission for necessary rent, assistance, and traveling
expenses. This is a very small sum. I know of no other way
in which the appropriation of so small a sum would result in
so large a benefit to the whole nation.

PRESIDENT THEODORE ROOSEVELT CONSERVATION TIME LINE[2]

1901

September 13

Roosevelt climbing Mount Marcy, the highest point in the Adirondacks, when a runner advised him that President McKinley had taken a turn for the worse from the assassin's bullet delivered on September 6.

September 14

President McKinley died; Roosevelt sworn in as President of the United States

December 3

First message to Congress; Roosevelt proclaimed: "The Forest and water problems are

---

[2] This time line is principally taken from information contained in the Encyclopedia of American Forest and Conservation History, Richard C. Davis Editor (Macmillan Pub. Co. 1983), Appendices 1 through 3. Other valuable resources include three websites, *About and Almanac of Theodore Roosevelt*, http://www.theodore-roosevelt.com/tr.html and *The Evolution of the Conservation Movement, 1850 – 1920*, http://memory.loc.gov/ammen/amrvhtml/conshome.html and Theodore Roosevelt Association website http://theodoreroosevelt.org /life/conservation.htm

I have taken certain liberties, as well. During the first part of Roosevelt's Presidency, National Forests were called "Forest Reserves." The term "National Forest" was not adopted until 1907. For purposes of the time line, "National Forest" is used throughout. Bird reserves eventually became known as National Wildlife Refuges. This modern term also is used unless there is a reason to do otherwise.

perhaps the most vital internal problems in the United States."

1902

April 11

San Isabel National Forest established Santa Rita National Forest established

April 16

Dismal River National Forest established; controlled experimentation in tree planting established at Dismal River National Forest

Niobrara National Forest established; experimentation in tree planting established at Niobrara National Forest

May 22

Medicine Bow National Forest established

Yellowstone National Forest acquired its name

Crater Lake National Park established

June 7

Alaska Game Act becomes law; adds protection for certain game animals

June 17

"Newlands" Reclamation Act becomes law; Act provides that receipts from sale and disposal of public lands in

	sixteen states will go toward financing irrigation works.
June 27	Minnesota National Forest established by act of congress and signed into law.
June 28	White River National Forest established
July 1	Platt Sulpher Springs Reservation established
July 2	Santa Catalina National Forest established
July 22	Mount Graham National Forest established
July 26	Lincoln National Forest established
July 30	Chiricahua National Forest established
August 16	Little Belt Mountains National Forest established
	Madison National Forest established
August 20	Alexander Archipelago National Forest established
September 4	Absaroka National Forest established
December 2	Second Annual Message to Congress. Roosevelt renews

request for wildlife protection in the forest reserves and again calls for reform of public land laws.

1903

January 9	Wind Cave National Park created
January 17	Luquillo National Forest established
January 29	Absaroka National Forest consolidated with Yellowstone National Forest; Absaroka National Forest name discontinued
	Teton National Forest combined with Yellowstone National Forest; Teton National Forest name discontinued
March 13	Roosevelt creates Committee on the Organization of Government Scientific Work. Committee results ultimately are used as a springboard for consolidation of forest management in the Department of Agriculture.
March 14	Pelican Island National Wildlife Refuge established

April 1	Roosevelt leaves for extended western tour
April 9 – 22	Roosevelt visits Yellowstone with John Burroughs
May 6	Roosevelt visits Grand Canyon
May 15 – 17	Roosevelt visits Yosemite with John Muir
May 29	Logan National Forest established
	Manti National Forest established
June 6	Western tour ends
June 9	Flathead National Forest consolidated with Lewis and Clarke National Forest; Flathead National Forest name discontinued
September 5	Pocatello National Forest established
October 2	Public Lands Commission appointed to report upon the condition, operation, and effect of existing land laws and to recommend appropriate changes
October 24	Aquarius National Forest established

December 7	Third Annual Message to Congress. President stresses need for land reform, protection of Alaska fisheries, and management reform
December 12	Highwood Mountains National Forest established
December 22	Santa Barbara National Forest created from Pine Mountain and Zaka Lake and Santa Ynez National Forests; Pine Mountain and Zaka Lake National Forest and Santa Ynez National Forest names discontinued

1904

February 5	Baker City National Forest established
March 5	Cave Hills National Forest established
	Slim Butte National Forest established
May 7	Grantsville National Forest established
May 26	Salt Lake National Forest established

June 2	Sullys Hill National Park established
October 4	Breton Island National Wildlife Refuge established
November 29	Modoc National Forest established
	Warner Mountains National Forest established
December 6	Fourth Annual Message to Congress. Roosevelt presents strong argument concerning the purpose and benefits of forest reserves and again requests management authority transferred to the Department of Agriculture. Message again calls for wildlife protection. The President also calls for a Yosemite National Park and a Grand Canyon National Park.

1905

January 24	Witchita National Wildlife Refuge established
February 1	Forest Transfer Act becomes law; administration of Forest Reserves (National Forests) transferred from Department of the Interior to the Department of Agriculture. Act establishes

	that money from sale and use of forest lands to be use for improvement and protection of National Forests
March 9	Stump Lake National Wildlife Refuge established
March 20	Pinal National Forest established
March 27	Plumas National Forest established
April 3	President leaves for Western hunting trip
April 26	Trinity National Forest established
May 5	Sevier National Forest established
May 6	Wallowa National Forest established
May 11	President returns from West
May 12	Chesnimnus National Forest established
	Elkhorn National Forest established
	Gunnison National Forest established
	Leadville National Forest established

Pike's PeakTimber Land
National Forest changed to
Pike's Peak National Forest
and Plum Creek and South
Platte National Forests added;
Plum Creek National Forest
and South Platte National
Forest names discontinued

Wenaha National Forest
established

May 23	Henrys Lake National Forest established
May 25	Weiser National Forest established
May 29	Sawtooth National Forest established
June 2	Wichita National Game Preserve established

Lassen Peak National Forest
established

Maury Mountain National
Forest established

June 3	Payette National Forest established
June 5	Uncompahgre National Forest established
June 12	Cassia National Forest established

Park Range National Forest established

Wet Mountains National Forest established

June 13   Cochetopah National Forest established

Montezuma National Forest established

July 14   Diamond Mountain National Forest established

July 21   Gila River National Forest renamed Gila National Forest

July 22   Short Pine National Forest established

July 25   Garden City National Forest established

August 25   Holy Cross National Forest established

September 25   Dixie National Forest established

October 3   Big Belt National Forest established

Hell Gate National Forest established

Lake Tahoe National Forest renamed Tahoe National Forest

Little Belt Mountains National
Forest renamed Little Belt

National Forest

Portales National Forest
established

Shasta National Forest
established

Tonto National Forest
established

October 10   Siskiwitt Islands National
                              Wildlife Refuge established

                              Huron Islands National
                              Wildlife Refuge established

                              Passage Key National Wildlife
                              Refuge established

October 12   Jemez National Forest
                              established

November 11   Yuba National Forest
                              established

December 5   Fifth Annual Message to
                              Congress. Roosevelt requests
                              reform of public land laws.
                              California is thanked for the
                              gift of the Yosemite Valley;
                              Congress is urged to accept the
                              gift and appropriate money for
                              a national park. Expansion of
                              Yellowstone National Park is
                              requested as well as the

creation of a sanctuary for bison.

1906

January 16	Uinta National Forest established
January 24	Beaver National Forest established
January 25	La Sal National Forest established
February 10	Indian Key Bird Reservation established
February 24	Fruita National Forest established
March 10	North Platte National Forest established
March 15	Blue Mountains National Forest established; portions of Baker City National Forest combined with Blue Mountains National Forest; the remainder is returned to public domain and the name Baker City National Forest is discontinued
April 12	Helena National Forest established

April 24	Vernon National Forest established
May 3	Ruby Mountains National Forest established
May 19	Fillmore National Forest established
May 28	Bear River National Forest established from consolidation of Logan National Forest and other lands; Logan National Forest name discontinued
June 8	American Antiquities Act becomes law; Act permits President to proclaim "monuments" for preservation of historic, prehistoric, and scientific attributes
June 11	Federal government accepts Yosemite Valley from California
June 25	Monterey National Forest established
	San Luis Obispo National Forest established
June 29	Grand Canyon Game Preserve authorized by Congress
	Mesa Verde National Monument designated
	Platt National Park established

July 18	Heppner National Forest established
	Pinnacles National Forest established
August 8	Grand Canon National Forest renamed Grand Canyon National Forest
August 10	Crazy Mountains National Forest established
August 13	Kootenai National Forest established
August 16	Wasatch National Forest established
August 21	Goose Lake National Forest established
September 17	Fremont National Forest established
	Tahoe National Forest increased through addition of Yuba National Forest and other lands; Yuba National Forest name discontinued
September 20	Lolo National Forest established
September 24	Devils Tower National Monument established
	Long Pine National Forest established

October 5	Siskiyou National Forest established
October 10	Siskiwit Islands National Wildlife Refuge designated
	Huron Islands National Wildlife Refuge designated
	Passage Key National Wildlife Refuge designated
	Indian Key National Wildlife Refuge designated
November 5	Baboquivari National Forest established
	Big Hole National Forest established
	Charleston National Forest established
	Gallinas National Forest established
	Ekalaka National Forest established
	Independence National Forest established
	Lemhi National Forest established
	Peloncillo National Forest established

Magdalena National Forest
established

Salmon River National Forest
established

San Mateo National Forest
established

Sierra Madre National Forest
established

Snowy Mountains National
Forest established

November 6

Coeur d'Alene National Forest
established

Huachuca National Forest
established

Manzano National Forest
established

Missoula National Forest
established

Pryor Mountains National
Forest established

Raft River National Forest
established

November 7

Taos National Forest
established

Tumacacori National Forest
established

November 28	Grand Canyon Game Preserve established by President's proclamation
December 3	Sixth Annual Message to Congress. President announces plan to stop Japanese raids on protected fur seal rookeries and to stop pelagic sealing
December 8	El Morro National Monument established
	Montezuma Castle National Monument established
	Petrified Forest National Monument established

1907

January 15	Caribou National Forest established
February 6	Big Burros National Forest established
	Glenwood National Forest established
	Monticello National Forest established
	Stony Creek National Forest established

February 22	Ouray National Forest established
March 1	Bear Lodge National Forest established
	Imnaha National Forest established through consolidation of Chesnimnus National Forest and Wallowa National Forest; Chisnimnus National Forest and Wallowa National Forest names discontinued;
	Coleville National Forest established
	Las AnimasNational Forest established
	Toiyabe National Forest established
March 2	Maury Mountain National Forest added to Blue Mountains National Forest
	Little Rockies National Forest established
	Cabinet National Forest established
	Cascade Range National Forest renamed Cascade National Forest and land added

Coquille National Forest
established

Lewis and Clarke National
Forest renamed Lewis and
Clark National Forest; land
added

Mount Rainier National Forest
renamed Rainier National
Forest

Maury Mountain National
Forest combined with Blue
Mountains National Forest;
Maury Mountain National
Forest name discontinued

Otter National Forest
established

Palouse National Forest
established

Port Neuf National Forest
established

Tillamook National Forest
established

Umpqua National Forest
established

March 4   Forest Reserves renamed
"National Forests"; President
is prohibited from creating
National Forests in six western
states

March 11	Chaco Canyon National Monument established
March 14	Roosevelt appoints Inland Waterways Commission to study river system of the United States including flood and erosion issues.
March 16	Designation of Portales National Forest rescinded
April 15	Monitor National Forest established
April 24	Sacramento National Forest created from part of Lincoln National Forest and other lands
May 6	Cinder Cone National Monument established
	Lassen Peak National Monument established
April 15	Toquima National Forest established
April 19	Guadalupe National Forest established
May 25	Dragoon National Forest established
	Inyo National Forest established
July 6	Trabuco Canon National Forest renamed Trabuco Canyon; land added

July 23	Chugach National Forest established
August 8	Tern Islands Imnaha National Forest established
August 17	Shell Keys Imnaha National Forest established
September 10	Tongass National Forest established
October 14	Three Arch Rocks Imnaha National Forest established
October 23	Flattery Rocks Imnaha National Forest established
	Copalis Rock Imnaha National Forest established
	Quillayute Needles Imnaha National Forest established
October 26	San Benito National Forest established
November 16	Gila Cliff Dwellings National Monument established
December 3	Seventh Annual Message to Congress. Roosevelt provides ringing endorsement of the Department of Agricultur's management of the forest reserves. Reform of public land laws again requested.
December 7	East Timbalier National Bird

	Reservation established
December 12	Vegas National Forest established
December 18	Arkansas National Forest established
December 19	Tonto National Monument established
December 30	Verde National Forest established

1908

January 9	Muir Woods National Monument established
January 11	Grand Canyon National Monument established
January 19	Pinal National Forest combined with Tonto National Forest; Pinal National Forest name discontinued
January 16	Pinnacles National Monument established
February 7	Jewel Cave National Monument established
February 24	Mosquito Island National Wildlife Refuge established
March 6	Ozark National Forest established

April 6	Tortugas National Wildlife Refuge established
April 16	Natural Bridges National Monument established
May 11	Lewis & Clark Cavern National Monument established
	Act for Protection of Game in Alaska becomes law
May 13-15	National Conference of Governors for purpose of addressing conservation of natural resources
May 15	Garden City National Forest renamed Kansas National Forest
May 23	Minnesota National Forest established
	National Bison Range established
June 8	National Conservation Commission appointed as a follow-up to Governors' Conference. The Commission is charged with inventorying national resources
June 18	Big Burros National Forest combined with Gila National Forest; Big Burros National Forest name discontinued

Datil National Forest created from a part of Gila National Forest and other lands

June 23   Grand Canyon National Game Preserve established

July 1   Absaroka National Forest reestablished from part of Yellowstone National Forest and all of Crazy Mountain National Forest; Crazy Mountain National Forest name discontinued

Afognak National Forest combined with Chugach National Forest

Alamo National Forest created through consolidation of Guadalupe and Sacramento National Forests; Sacramento National Forest name discontinued

Alexander Archipelago National Forest combined with Tongas National Forest; Alexander Archipelago National Forest name discontinued

Angeles National Forest created from San Bernardino National Forest and parts of Santa Barbara and San Gabriel National Forests; San

Bernardino National Forest
name discontinued

Apache National Forest
established from portion of
Black Mesa National Forest

Aquarius National Forest
renamed Powell National
Forest

Arapaho National Forest
established from parts of
Medicine Bow, Pikes Peak,
and Leadville National Forests

Crater National Forest
established from Ashland
National Forest and other
forest land

Ashley National Forest created
from part of the Unita National
Forest

Garces National Forest created
from Baboquivari, Huachuca,
and Tumacacori National
Forests

Battlement National Forest
created from part of
Battlement Mesa National
Forest; remainder of
Battlement Mesa National
Forest combined with Holy
Cross National Forest;
Battlement Mesa National
Forest name discontinued

Bear Lodge National Forest
combined with part of Black
Hills National Forest to create
Sundance National Forest;
Bear Lodge National Forest
name discontinued

Bear River National Forest
divided between Pocatello
National Forest and Cache
National Forest; Bear River
National Forest name discon-
tinued

Beartooth National Forest
established from Pryor
Mountains National Forest and
a portion of Yellowstone
National Forest; Pryor
Mountains National Forest
name discontinued

Beaver National Forest
combined with Fillmore
National Forest; Beaver
National Forest name discontinued

Beaverhead National Forest
from portions of Big Hole,
Bitter Root, and Hell Gate
National Forests

Big Belt National Forest
divided between Gallatin and
Helena National Forests and
the name Big Belt National
Forest discontinued

Big Hole National Forest
divided among Beaverhead,
Deerlodge, and Bitterroot
National Forests; Big Hole
National Forest discontinued

Deerlodge National Forest
created from parts of Big Hole
and Hell Gate National Forests

Big Horn National Forest
changed to Bighorn National
Forest

Bitter Root National Forest
changed to Bitterroot with
lands added from Hell Gate
and and Big Hole National
Forests and lands transferred to
Beaverhead, Clearwater,
Nezperce, and Salmon
National Forests

Black Mesa National Forest
lands divided among
Sitgreaves, Tonto, Apache, and
Coconino National Forests;
Black Mesa National Forest
name discontinued

Blackfeet National Forest
created from part of Lewis and
Clark National Forest

Blue Mountains National
Forest lands dispersed among
Whitman, Malheur, Umatilla,
and Deschutes National

Forests; Blue Mountains
National Forest name discontinued

Boise National Forest
established from part of
Sawtooth National Forest

Bonneville National Forest
created from part of Yellowstone National Forest

Oregon National Forest created
from part of Cascade National
Forest and all of Bull Run
National Forest; Bull Run
National Forest name discontinued

Cache National Forest created
from a portion of Bear River
National Forest

California National Forest
created from a portion of
Trinity and Stony Creek
National Forests

Carson National Forest created
from Taos National Forest and
a portion of Jemez National
Forest; Taos National Forest
name discontinued

Minidoka National Forest
created from Raft River and
Cassia National Forests; Cassia
National Forest and Raft River

National Forest names discontinued

Cave Hills National Forest added to Sioux National Forest; Cave Hills National Forest name discontinued

Challis National Forest established from parts of Salmon River and Sawtooth National Forests

Charleston National Forest added to Moapa National Forest; Charleston National Forest name discontinued

Chelan National Forest created from part of Washington National Forest

Cheyenne National Forest created from Crow Creek National Forest and a portion of Medicine Bow National Forest; Crow Creek National Forest name discontinued

Peloncillo National Forest added to Chiracahua National Forest; Pelloncillo National Forest name discontinued

Afognak National Forest added to Chugach National Forest

Clearwater National Forest established from parts of

Coeur d' Alene and Bitter Root
National Forests

Cleveland National Forest
created from San Jacinto and
Trabuco Canyon; San Jacinto
National Forest and Trabuco
Canyon National Forest names
discontinued

Cochetopa National Forest
changed from Cochetopah
National Forest

Coconino National Forest
created from parts of Tonto,
Black Mesa, and Grand
Canyon National Forest as
well as all of San Franciso
Mountains National Forest;
San Francisco Mountains
National Forest and San
Gabriel National Forest names
discontinued

Palouse National Forest added
to Coeur d' Alene National
Forest; Palouse National Forest
name discontinued

Columbia National Forest
created from a portion of
Rainier National Forest

Coquille National Forest
combined with Siskiyou
National Forest; Coquille

National Forest name discontinued

Coronado National Forest established by consolidation of Dragoon, Santa Catalina, and Santa Rita National Forests; Dragoon National Forest, Santa Rita National Forest, and Santa Catalina National Forest names discontinued

Crook National Forest created from parts of Tonto and Mount Graham National Forests as well as other lands; remainder of Mount Graham National Forest is returned to public lands; Mount Graham National Forest name discontinued

Otter National Forest renamed Custer National Forest

Deschutes National Forest created from parts of Blue Mountains, Cascades, and Fremont National Forests

Diamond Mountains National Forest divided amongst Plumas and Lassen National Forests; Diamond Mountains National Forest name discontinued

Dismal River National Forest transferred to Nebraska National Forest

Ekalaka National Forest added
to Sioux National Forest;
Ekalaka National Forest name
discontinued

Elkhorn National Forest
combined with Helena
National Forest; Elkhorn
National Forest name discontinued

Fish Lake National Forest
changed to Fishlake National
Forest; Glenwood National
Forest added to Fishlake
National Forest; Glenwood
National Forest name discon-
tinued

Flathead National Forest
reestablished from a portion of
Lewis and Clark National
Forest

Goose Lake National Forest
added to Fremont National
Forest; Goose Lake National
Forest name discontinued

Fruita National Forest
combined with Uncompahgre
National Forest; Fruita
National Forest name discontinued

Gallatin National Forest gains
a portion of Big Belt National
Forest

Gallinas National Forest transferred to Lincoln National Forest; Gallinas National Forest name discontinued

Garces National Forest created by consolidation of Baboquivari, Huachuca, and Tumacacori National Forests; Huachaci National Forest and Tumacacori National Forest names discontinued

Grand Canyon National Forest combined with Coconuno and Kaibab National Forests; Kaibab National Forest established; a portion of Grand Canyon National Forest returned to public lands; Grand Canyon National Forest name discontinued

Grantsville National Forest combined with Wasatch National Forest; Grantsville National Forest name discontinued

Guadalupe National Forest combined with Alamo National Forest; Guadalupe National Forest name discontinued

Hayden National Forest created from all of Sierra Madre National Forest and a portion of Park Range National Forest; Sierra Madre National Forest name discontinued

Hell Gate National Forest divided among Beaverhead, Deerlodge, Missoula, and Bitterroot National Forests; Hell Gate National Forest name discontinued

Henrys Lake National Forest combined with a portion of Yellowstone National Forest to create Targhee National Forest; Henrys Lake National Forest name discontinued

Heppner National Forest combined with portion of Blue Mountains National Forest to create Umatilla National Forest; Heppner National Forest name discontinued

Highwood Mountains National Forest combined with Little Belt, Snowy Mountains, and Little Rockies National Forests to create Jefferson National Forest; Highwood Mountains National Forest, Little Rockies National Forest, Snowy Mountains National Forest, and Little Belt National Forest names discontinued

Humbolt National Forest
created by consolidation of
Independence and Ruby
Mountains National Forests;
Independence National Forest
and Ruby Mountains National
Forest names discontinued

Idaho National Forest
established from part of
Payette National Forest

Imnaha National Forest
renamed Wallowa National
Forest

Kaniksu National Forest
created from part of Priest
River National Forest

La Sal National Forest
combined with Monticello
National Forest to create La
Salle National Forest; La Sal
National Forest name dis-
continued

Lassen Peak National Forest
renamed Lassen National
Forest; lands transferred to and
from Plumas, Shasta and
Diamond Mountain National
Forests

Long Pine National Forest
combined with Sioux National
Forest; Long Pine National
Forest name discontinued

San Mateo National Forest
added to Magdalena National
Forest

Malheur National Forest
created from part of Blue
Mountains National Forest

Mount Taylor National Forest
and other lands added to
Manzano National Forest

Moapa National Forest created
through consolidation of
Charleston and Vegas National
Forests

Warner Mountains National
Forest to Modoc National
Forest; Warner Mountains
National Forest name dis-
continued

Monitor National Forest added
to Toiyabe National Forest;
Monitor National Forest name
discontinued

Mono National Forest created
from parts of Inyo, Sierra,
Stanislaus, and Tahoe National
Forests

Nebo National Forest created
by consolidation of Payson and
Vernon National Forests and a
portion of Fillmore National
Forest; Payson National Forest

and Vernon National Forest
names discontinued

Nebraska National Forest
created by consolidation of
Dismal River, Niobrara, and
North Platte National Forests;
North Platte National Forest
and Niobrara National Forest
names discontinued

Nezperce National Forest
created from parts of Bitter
Root and Weiser National
Forests

Oregon National Forest
established from part of
Cascade National Forest and
all of Bull Run National Forest

Ouray National Forest divided
between Montezuma and
Uncompahgre National
Forests; Ouray National Forest
name discontinued

Park Range National Forest
divided between Routt and
Hayden National Forests; Park
Range National Forest name
discontinued

Pecos Ricer National Forest
renamed Pecos National Forest

Pend d'Oreille National Forest
created from parts of Cabinet,

Coeur d' Alene, Kootenai, and
Priest River National Forests

Pike's Peak National Forest
renamed Pike National Forest

Pinnicles National Forest
added to Monterey National
Forest; Pinnicles National
Forest name discontinued

Pocatello National Forest
increased through addition of
parts of Bear River and Port
Neuf National Forests; Bear
River National Forest and Port
Neuf National Forest names
discontinued

Prescott National Forest
increased through addition of
Verde National Forest; Verde
National Forest name discontinued

Priest River National Forest
divided to form Pend d'Oreille
and Kaniksu National Forests;
Priest River National Forest
name discontinued

Rio Grande National Forest
established from parts of San
Juan and Cochetopa National
Forests

Routt National Forest formed
from part of Park Range
National Forest

Salmon National Forest
created from parts of Bitter
Root, Lemhi, and Salmon
River National Forests;
Salmon River National Forest
name discontinued

Salt Lake National Forest
combined with Wasatch
National Forest; Salt Lake
National Forest name dis-
continued

San Benito National Forest
added to Monterey National
Forest; San Benito National
Forest name discontinued

San Isabel National Forest
increased through addition of
Wet Mountains National
Forest; Wet Mountains
National Forest name
discontinued

San Luis National Forest
created from part of San Luis
Obispo National Forest; San
Luis Obispo National Forest
name discontinued

San Mateo National Forest
added to Magdalena National
Forest; San Mateo National
Forest name discontinued

Santa Barbara National Forest
increased through additions of

San Luis Obispo National
Forest and part of San Gabriel
National Forest

Sequoia National Forest
created from a portion of
Sierra National Forest

Short Pine National Forest
transferred to Sioux National
Forest; Short Pine National
Forest name discontinued

Shoshone National Forest
created from part of Yellowstone National Forest

Sioux National Forest created
through consolidation of Cave
Hills, Ekalaka, Long Pine,
Short Pine, and Slim Butte
National Forests; Slim Butte
National Forest name
discontinued

Siskiyou National Forest
increased through addition of
Coquille National Forest and
other lands

Sitgreaves National Forest
created from parts of Black
Mesa and Tonto National
Forests

Siuslaw National Forest
created from parts of
Tillamook and Umpqua
National Forests

Snoquaimie National Forest
established

Stony Creek National Forest
transferred to Trinity National
Forest; Stony Creek National
Forest name discontinued

Sundance National Forest
created from Bear Lodge and
part of Black Hills National
Forests

Targhee National Forest
established from Yellowstone
National Forest and all of
Henrys Lake National Forest

Teton National Forest
restablished from portion of
Yellowstone National Forest

Tillamook National Forest
partially combined with
Umpqua National Forest to
form Siuslaw National Forest;
remainder returned to public
lands; Tillamook National
Forest name discontinued

Toiyabe National Forest
increased through the addition
of Monitor and Toquima
National Forests; Toquimq
National Forest name dis-
continued

Tongas National Forest
increased through addition of

Alexander Archipelago
National Forest

Umatilla National Forest
created from part of Blue
Mountains National Forest and
all of Heppner National Forest

Wenatchee National Forest
established from part of
Washington National Forest

Whitman National Forest
established from part of Blue
Mountains National Forest

Wyoming National Forest
established from part of
Yellowstone National Forest

August 8	Key West National Wildlife Refuge established
	Klamath Lake National Wildlife Refuge established
August 18	Lake Malheur National Wildlife Refuge established
August 28	Chase Lake National Wildlife Refuge established
September 15	Pine Island National Wildlife Refuge established
	Tumacacori National Monument established

September 26	Matlacha Pass National Wildlife Refuge established
	Palma Sola National Wildlife Refuge established
October 23	Island Bay National Wildlife Refuge established
October 26	Loch-Katrine National Wildlife Refuge established
November 24	Dakota National Forest established
	Ocala National Forest established
November 27	Choctawhatchee National Forest established
December 7	Wheeler National Monument established
December 8	Eighth Annual Message to Congress. Roosevelt stresses need to guard against erosion brought about through deforestation and requests a better system of managing national parks
December -	Roosevelt hosts Joint Conservation Conference (aka "Second Governor's Conference")

1909

February 3	Hawaiian Islands National Wildlife Refuge established
February 10	Marquette National Forest established
	Nevada National Forest established
February 13	Superior National Forest established
February 18	Roosevelt hosts North American Conservation Conference attended by representatives of Canada, Newfoundland, Mexico, and the United States.
February 23	Magdalena National Forest and other lands added to Datil National Forest; Magdalena National Forest name discontinued
February 25	Salt River National Wildlife Refuge established
	East Park National Wildlife Refuge established
	Deer Flat National Wildlife Refuge established
	Willow Creek National Wildlife Refuge established

Carlsbad National Wildlife
Refuge established

Rio Grande National Wildlife
Refuge established

Cold Springs National Wildlife
Refuge established

Belle Fourche National
Wildlife Refuge established

Strawberry Valley National
Wildlife Refuge established

Keechelus National Wildlife
Refuge established

Kachess National Wildlife
Refuge established

Clealum National Wildlife
Refuge established

Bumping Lake National
Wildlife Refuge established

Conconully National Wildlife
Refuge established

Pathfinder National Wildlife
Refuge established

Shoshone National Wildlife
Refuge established

Minidoka National Wildlife
Refuge established

February 27	Tuxedni National Wildlife Refuge established
	Saint Lazaria National Wildlife Refuge established
	Yukon Delta National Wildlife Refuge established
	Culebra National Wildlife Refuge established
	Farallon National Wildlife Refuge established
	Bering Sea National Wildlife Refuge established
	Pribilof National Wildlife Refuge established
	Bogoslof National Wildlife Refuge established
	Fire Island National Wildlife Refuge established
March 2	Mount Olympus National Monument established
	Zuni National Forest established
March 4	Presidential term of Theodore Roosevelt ends

ENDNOTES

Preface

[1] Thayer, William Roscoe, Theodore Roosevelt An Intimate Biography (Houghton Mifflin Co, 1919), 272.

[2] Pinchot, Gifford, Breaking New Ground (Island Press 1998), 314.

[3] Pinchot, Gifford, Breaking New Ground (Island Press 1998), 314.

[4] Thayer, William Roscoe, Theodore Roosevelt An Intimate Biography (Houghton Mifflin Co, 1919), 262-63.

[5] Muir, John, Our National Parks (Houghton Mifflin Co. 1901), at 361

[6] Pinchot, Gifford, Breaking New Ground (Island Press 1998), at 345.

Teddy Roosevelt – A Pioneer Conservationist

[1] Pinchot, Gifford, Breaking New Ground (Island Press 1998), at 145.

[2] Burroughs, John, Camping *with the President,* 97 The Atlantic Monthly 585 (May 1906).

[3] The success of the club so overwhelmed him (50,000 members), Grinnell had to disband it in 1889. State chapters continued independently until the present National Audubon Society was formed in 1905. Thus, the Boone and Crockett Club is the oldest national organization committed to wildlife and habitat preservation. Rieger, John F., American

Sportsmen and the Origins of Conservation (Winchester Press 1975).

[4] Burroughs, John, Camping *with the President,* 97 The Atlantic Monthly 585 (May 1906).

[5] Rieger, John F., American Sportsmen and the Origins of Conservation (Winchester Press 1975).

[6] Morison, Elting E., Vol. 2 The Letters of Theodore Roosevelt (Harvard Univ. Press 1951), at 1157.

[7] An Old Acquaintance, *The Personality of President Roosevelt,* Century (Nov. 1901).

[8] Pinchot, Gifford, Breaking New Ground (Island Press 1998), at 345.

[9] Roosevelt, Theodore, An Autobiography (1913), Ch. XI.

[10] Roosevelt, Theodore, An Autobiography (1913), Ch. XI.

[11] Pinchot, Gifford, Breaking New Ground (Island Press 1998), at 353.

[12] Cutright, Paul Russell, Theodore Roosevelt – The Making of a Conservationist ((Univ. of Illinois Press 1985), at 212.

[13] Harbaugh, William Henry, Power and Responsibility – The Life and Times of Theodore Roosevelt (Farr, Straus, & Cudahy 1961) at 320.

[14] Harbaugh, William Henry, Power and Responsibility – The Life and Times of Theodore Roosevelt (Farr, Straus, & Cudahy 1961), at 324.

[15] Roosevelt, Theodore, December 3, 1907 Message to Congress.

[16] Muir, John, Our National Parks (Houghton Mifflin Co. 1891), at 364 - 65.

[17] Peffer, E. Louise, The Closing of the Public Domain (Stanford Univ. Press 1951) at 8.

[18] Wilkinson, Charles F. and Anderson, H. Michael, Land and Resource Planning in the National Forests (Island Press 1987), at 47.

[19] Rieger, John F., American Sportsmen and the Origins of Conservation (Winchester Press1975).

[20] Harbaugh, William Henry, Power and Responsibility – The Life and Times of Theodore Roosevelt (Farr, Straus, & Cudahy 1961), at 326.

[21] Harbaugh, William Henry, Power and Responsibility – The Life and Times of Theodore Roosevelt (Farr, Straus, & Cudahy 1961), at 331. This was a method of analysis the President apparently enjoyed. Several years later, frustrated that Congress mandated a seven man commission to oversee work on the Panama canal, Roosevelt used the same analysis to make one commission member superior to all others:"[His] efforts to work under the law...were so unsuccessful that he resolved to assume powers which the law did not give him but which he did not forbid him to exercise." "McCullough, David, The Path Between the Seas – The Creation of the Panama Canal 1870-1914 (Simon and Schuster 1977), at 510.

[22] Ponder, Stephen, Managing the Press (St. Martin's Press1998), at 30.

[23] *Ibid.*

[24] *Ibid.*, at 21.

[25] Morison, Elting E., Vol. 5, The Letters of Theodore Roosevelt (Harvard Univ. Press 1951), at 793.

[26] Senator Thomas C. Platt was the powerful New York Republican party boss who orchestrated efforts to "bury" Roosevelt in the vice presidency.

[27] Roosevelt, Theodore, XX The Works of Theodore Roosevelt – An Autobiography (Charles Scribner & Sons 1925), at 275.

[28] Fox, Stephen, John Muir and His Legacy (Little, Brown and Company 1981), at 129.

[29] Gould, Lewis L., The Presidency of Theodore Roosevelt (Univ. Press of Kansas 1991), at 11. In his delightful work, *Theodore Roosevelt, The Making of a Conservationist*, author Paul Russell Cutright. writes about another aspect of the Bully Pulpit, Roosevelt's tendency to write articles for popular magazines. Like Ronald Regan years later, Roosevelt was able to take his message directly to the people. As his presidency progressed, he increasingly had to go to the people. As noted by Cutright:

> During his tenure as president, Theodore Roosevelt entertained more naturalists at the White House than any president before or since; but the naturalists he enjoyed most, and therefore entertained oftener, were also writers and conservationists....
>
> Roosevelt's interest in the naturalists/ writers/conservationists went beyond having them at a luncheon...If he learned that one of them had a manuscript in preparation, he often agreed to read it critically. If another asked him to write a forward, he agreed; if still another produced a book he liked, he wrote a favorable review of it for *Outlook* or the *New York Times*

Cutright, Paul Russell, Theodore Roosevelt – The Making of a Conservationist ((Univ. of Illinois Press 1985), at 239.

[30] Ponder, Stephen, Managing the Press (St. Martin's Press 1998), at 41. As noted by Louise Peffer:

> Roosevelt had been aided immeasurably in building up public opinion in support of his program by the commissions created during his years in the White House. The Public Lands Commission, the Inland Waterways Commission, and the Conservation Commission were prominent among them. [By the end of Roosevelt's administration,] Congress was tired of commissions. ... Congress was resentful at being forced unwillingly to act in accordance with the dictates of the public opinion aroused by these commissions.

Peffer, at 108-09. Weary of Roosevelt's successful use of the bully pulpit, in 1909 Congress adopted a bill forbidding public money for commissions unless it authorized them. The bill further prohibited executive employees from doing detailed work for the commissions.

[31] Opening Address of the President, Proceedings of a Conference of Governors.

[32] Encyclopedia of American Forest and Conservation History, Richard C. Davis, Editor (MacmillianPub. Co. 1983), at 98.

[33] Encyclopedia of American Forest and Conservation History, Richard C. Davis, Editor (MacmillianPub. Co. 1983), at 98.

[34] Roosevelt, Theodore, XX The Works of Theodore Roosevelt – An Autobiography (Charles Scribner & Sons 1925).

[35] *Ibid.*

[36] "Though bold and impulsive, in important matters he was calculating and deliberate. Guided by an uncompromising moralism, Roosevelt was nonetheless a savvy and pragmatic politician." Hanson, David C., Theodore Roosevelt: Lion in the White House, http://www.virginiawestern. edu/vwhansd//HIS122/TR_Lion.html

[37] Morison, Elting E., Vol. 3, The Letters of Theodore Roosevelt (Harvard Univ. Press 1951), at 629-630.

[38] *Ibid.*

[39] Ponder, Stephen, Managing the Press (St. Martin's Press1998), at 37.

[40] Morison, Elting E., Vol. 3, The Letters of Theodore Roosevelt (Harvard Univ. Press 1951), at 629-630

[41] Pinchot, Gifford, Breaking New Ground (Island Press 1998), at 243-44.

[42] Williams, Gerald, W., *Early Years of National Forest Management: Implications of the Organic Act of 1897,* http://fs.jorge.com/archives/History_National/1897Or ganicActESAPaper.htm

[43] Roosevelt, Theodore, Outdoor Pastimes of an American Hunter (Forest & Stream Pub. Co. 1990).

[44] Harbaugh, William Henry, Power and Responsibility – The Life and Times of Theodore Roosevelt (Farr, Straus, & Cudahy 1961), at 330.

[45] Morison, Elting. E., Vol. 4, The letters of Theodore Roosevelt (Harvard Univ. Press 1951), at 1127, n.3.

[46] Ise, John, The United States Forest Policy (Yale Univ. Press 1924), 155.

[47] In 1907, the Division of Forestry was renamed the Forest Service.

[48] Pinchot, Gifford, Breaking New Ground (Island Press 1998), at 201.

Roosevelt's Conservation Philosophy

[49] Miller, Char, Gifford Pinchot and the Making of Modern Environmentalism (Island Press 2002), at 124.

[50] Reiger, John F., American Sportsmen and the Origins of Conservation (Winchester Press1975), at 85.

[51] Pinchot's followers remain fervent today. As noted by Edgar B. Brannon, Jr. in forward to Harold K. Steen's book, The Conservation Diaries of Gifford Pinchot:

> He [Pinchot] is an icon, an abbreviated version of the man who actually existed in the flesh and blood. We have recreated Gifford to serve our own needs. The Gifford Pinchot of the second century of conservation is very modern in his thinking, politically correct, and ecologically versed. Every one of his statements is biblical. His populist values and beliefs are the core beliefs of our institutions.

Steen, Harold K., The Conservation Diaries of Gifford Pinchot (Forest History Society 2001)(forward).

[52] Pinchot, Gifford, The Fight for Conservation (Doubleday, Page & Co. 1910), at 133.

[53] Pinchot, Gifford, The Fight for Conservation (Doubleday, Page & Co. 1910), at 42. Pinchot may have been correct is stating that there was "misconception" as to his definition of conservation. However, for almost a decade – 1890 to 1897 – forest policy leaned toward preservation of forest reserves. Two of the first forest reserves created by Congress were actually set aside as national parks. The first forest preserve set aside by presidential executive order was the Yellowstone reserve intended as a supplementary protection of Yellowstone National Park. It was not until 1897 that Congress refined reserve policy, stipulating that forest reserves were intended to ensure sustainable timber harvests and protect water resources.

[54] Pinchot, Gifford, The Fight for Conservation (Doubleday, Page & Co. 1910), at 44 – 48.

[55] Pinchot, Gifford, The Fight for Conservation (Doubleday, Page & Co. 1910), at 48.

[56] There does come a time when Muir becomes fatigued and angered with the puffery and sanctimony of Pinchot who appears (to Muir) to violate all of the standards of conservationism and preservationism in order to strong-arm passage of the Hetch Hetchy dam. Noted Muir: "Nature's sublime wonderlands, the admiration and joy of the world. Nevertheless ... from the very beginning, however well guarded, they have always been subject to attack by despoiling gain seekers and mischief-makers of every degree from Satan to Senators, eagerly trying to make everything immediately and selfishly commercial with schemes disguised in smug-smiling philanthropy, industriously, sham piously crying, 'Conservation, conservation, panutilization,' that man and beast may be fed and the dear Nation made great." Muir, John,

The Yosemite, *published in* John Muir – The Eight Wilderness – Discovery Books (Diadem Books 1992), at 714.

[57] Steen, Harold K., The Conservation Diaries of Gifford Pinchot (The Forest History Society 2001), at 162. This comment is all the more harsh when one considers that these "nature lovers" included people Pinchot once called mentor, colleague, and friend – John Muir, John Singer Sargent, and George Bird Grinnell.

Part of the problem with Pinchot's definition of conservation was that it was an attempt to ignore or Shanghai congressional policy. Pinchot claimed that "conservation" was nothing more than an extension of his forestry program. However, the Congress mandated that forest reserves were principally for timber and water protection with certain other uses allowed; in the forest reserves his working definition and Congressional policy were consistent. No such use policy was articulated as to national parks. To impose the utilitarian policy upon parks simply was not justified. As noted by Robert Underwood Johnson during testimony before the Senate Committee on Public Lands, parks are different than forest reserves.

[58] One definition is that preservationist are persons who want to keep nature and wildlife untouched by man. Reiger, John F., American Sportsmen and the Origins of Conservation (Winchester Press 1975), at 45. Certainly this was not Muir's position. He too supported wise use. Like Grinnell and Roosevelt, Muir recognized that certain uses were incompatible with the highest use of the environment.

[59] Muir, John, Our National Parks, (emphasis by author, not by Muir) *published in* John Muir – The Eight Wilderness – Discovery Books (Diadem Books 1992).

[60] This purpose was changed to protecting the mountains and other natural wonders in 1951.

[61] Muir, John, Our National Parks, (emphasis by author, not by Muir) *published in* John Muir – The Eight Wilderness – Discovery Books (Diadem Books 1992), at 593.

[62] Muir, John, Our National Parks, (*published in* John Muir – The Eight Wilderness – Discovery Books (Diadem Books 1992), at 594. If the arguments of his close friends are any indication, Muir also did not favor absolute preservation if true human needs were at issue. In a June 25, 1913 letter presented to the House Committee on Public Lands, Muir compatriot Robert Underwood Johnson stated: "The opponents of the Hetch Hetchy scheme maintain that their position is not inimical to the true interests of San Francisco. They say that if there were no other source of good and abundant water for the city they would willingly sacrifice the valley to the lives and health of its citizens." Similarly, the Sierra Club Bulletin, vol., IX, No. 3 (January 1914) stated in an editorial: "Had this [the damming of Hetch Hetchy] been done under spur of a real public necessity it would not be a serious matter. The Sierra Club has always stood ready to approve the diversion of any part of the Yosemite National Park if it could be shown that it was the only place from which San Francisco can derive a satisfactory supply of water."

[63] Both Roosevelt and Muir compared aspects of Yosemite to cathedrals.

[64] Wilkinson, Charles F. and Anderson, H. Michael, Land and Resource Planning in the National Forests (Island Press 1987), at 134 *quoting* 1908 Annual Report of the Chief Forester at 15. Pinchot biographer Char Miller tells us that Pinchot altered his strict view late in life. In the fourth edition of The Making of a Forester, Pinchot noted that not all of the good which the forest offers can be measured in board feet, cods, and dollars and cents. "It is immeasurable because it reaches and uplifts our inner selves." Miller, Char, Gifford Pinchot and the Making of Modern Environmentalism (Island Press 2001), at 338. This "conversion" is not reflected in Pinchot's subsequent book Breaking New Ground.

[65] Miller, Char, Gifford Pinchot and the Making of Modern Environmentalism (Island Press 2002), at 85.

[66] Muir, John, Our National Parks, (emphasis by author, not by Muir) *published in* John Muir – The Eight Wilderness – Discovery Books (Diadem Books 1992), at 459.

[67] Muir, John, Our National Parks, (emphasis by author, not by Muir) *published in* John Muir – The Eight Wilderness – Discovery Books (Diadem Books 1992), at 491.

[68] Roosevelt, Theodore, An Autobiography (1913), at chapter Ch. XI.

[69] Reiger, John F., American Sportsmen and the Origins of Conservation (Winchester Press1975), at 85. The preserve was established in 1885, the year after Roosevelt took a leave from politics following the deaths of his mother and his wife.

[70] Pinchot, Gifford, *Breaking New Ground* (Island Press 1998), at 26-27. This was written after Pinchot's supposed conversion." See footnote 10.

[71] Bade, William Frederick, *The Life and Letters of John Muir* (Houghton Mifflin Co. 1924).

[72] Roosevelt, Theodore, *Outdoor Pastimes of an American Hunter* (1905).

[73] It appears that he was careful to choose locations unsuitable for human consumptive purposes. In this way, he managed to reduce his exposure to political or legal challenge. However, these reserves were without financing. Unless the growing Audubon Society provided funds, many remained paper reserves.

[74] Grinnell, George Bird (editor), *American Big Game in its Haunts; The Book of the Boone and Crockett Club* (Forest and Stream Publishing Co. 1904), printed at http://memory.loc.gov/cgi-bin/query/r?ammem/consrvbib:@FIELD(NUMBERv g01))

[75] At this time, the phrase "forest reserves" was broad enough to encompass national parks, wildlife refuges, and today's national forests.

[76] *Ibid.*

[77] *Ibid.* (emphasis added). The legal and political restraints placed upon Roosevelt also are evident in this passage. Preservation cannot occur without the backing of the people. As Roosevelt once professed to John Muir: "I will do everything in my power to protect not only the Yosemite, which we already have protected, but other similar great natural beauties of this country. But you must remember that it is out of

the question permanently to protect them unless we have a certain degree of friendliness toward them on the part of the people of the State in which they are situated." Morison, Elting E., Vol. 5, The Letters of Theodore Roosevelt (Harvard Univ. Press 1951), at 793.

[78] *A National Park Service,* The Outlook (February 3, 1912).

[79] *The Preservation of Niagara Falls,* The Outlook (February 3, 1912).

[80] Roosevelt, Theodore, A Book-Lover's Holliday in the Open.

The First Term 1901 - 1905

[81] Roosevelt did not directly speak to Congress. Back then, the State of the Union message, as it is now called, was delivered to Congress and read by staff.

[82] Wilkinson, Charles F. and Anderson, H. Michael, Land and Resource Planning in the National Forests (Island Press 1987), at 53

[83] Pinchot, Gifford, Breaking New Ground, at 198.

[84] *Ibid.* at 199 – 200.

[85] *Ibid.* at 201 - 202.

[86] Friends of Crater Lake National Park, Newsletter, Vol. 4., No. 4 (Fall 1999).

[87] Morison, Elting E., Vol. 2 The Letters of Theodore Roosevelt (Harvard Univ. Press 1951), at 1292.

[88] Theodore Roosevelt's Letters to His Children

[89] Roosevelt, Theodore, Outdoor Pastimes of an American Hunter (1990).

[90] *Ibid.* Several years later, the Hetch Hetchy controversy in the park had matured to full bloom. Whether to dam a portion of the Yosemite National Park to provide water and power to San Francisco was before the federal government. Roosevelt had left office, replaced by his successor the 300 plus, pound William Taft. Taft traveled to Yosemite to view it and the Hetch Hetchy Valley. A day trip with John Muir culminated at a hotel. Again the courtiers prepared the feast within the warm and beckoning hotel. Muir invited the rotund president to travel on and camp in the valley. The priorities and beckoning calls were different for the new President. He bade Muir good night.

[91] Fox, Stephen, John Muir and His Legacy (Little, Brow and Company 1981), at 126.

[92] *Ibid.*

[93] Morison, Elting E., The Letters of Theodore Roosevelt (Harvard Univ. Press 1951), at 1183, n. 1.

[94] Roosevelt, Theodore, A Book-Lover's Holidays in the Open (Bartleby.com 1916)

[95] Office of Communications, USDA Forest Service, *The Forest Service in 1905: Change In Management of the Forest Reserves* (1999), http://fs.jorge.com/archives/History_National/1905 TransferAct.htm

[96] Morison, Elting E., Vol. 5, The Letters of Theodore Roosevelt (Harvard Univ. Press 1952), at 99.

[97] *U.S. v. Grimaud,* 220 U.S. 506, 522 (1911).

The Second Term 1905 - 1909

[98] Lee, Ronald F., The Antiquities Act of 1906 (January 19, 2001, Park Net), at Ch. 6. http://www.cr.nps.gov/aad/pubs/INDEX.HTM.

[99] Lee, at Ch. 6.

[100] Pinchot, Gifford, Breaking New Ground (Island Press 1998), at 299-300.

[101] Morison, Elting, E., Vol. 5, The Letters of Theodore Roosevelt (Harvard Univ. Press 1952), at 604.

[102] Pinchot, at 300.

[103] Morison, Elting, E., Vol. 5, The Letters of Theodore Roosevelt (Harvard Univ. Press 1952), at 838 (Invitation to Alabama Governor Braxton Bragg Comer).

[104] *Ibid.*

[105] The Conference demonstrated to the Governors the advantages of such meetings and they have been meeting as a group every year since.

9. Morison, Elting E., Vol. 6, The Papers of Theodore Roosevelt (Harvard Univ. Press 1952), at 1065-66.

[107] *Ibid.*

[108] In 1950, Monument status of Wheeler was revoked and the land was transferred to the Forest Service. It now is maintained as part the Wheeler Geologic Area within the Rio Grande National Forest.

National Forests

[109] Wilkinson, Charles F. and Anderson, H. Michael, Land and Resource Planning in the National Forests (Island

Press 1987), at 17 *quoting* Annual Report of the Secretary of the Interior, H.R. Exec. Doc. No. 1, 45th Cong., 2d Sess., pt. 5 (1877).

[110] Muir, John Our National Parks (Houghton Mifflin Co. 1891), at 362.

[111] U.S. Stats. at Large, vol. 26, Chap. 561, pp. 1095-1103; H.R. 7254, § 24. The Act is now commonly referred to as the Forest Reserve Act of 1891. Steen, Harold, K., *The Beginning of the National Forest System,* printed in American Forests, Nature, Culture, and Politics (University of Kansas Press 1997)(Char Miller editor).

[112] Muir, John Our National Parks (Houghton Mifflin Co. 1891), at 363.

[113] Steen, Harold, K., *The Beginning of the National Forest System,* printed in American Forests, Nature, Culture, and Politics (University of Kansas Press 1997)(Char Miller editor).

[114] Steen, Harold, K., *The Beginning of the National Forest System,* printed in American Forests, Nature, Culture, and Politics (University of Kansas Press 1997)(Char Miller editor).

[115] Muir, John Our National Parks (Houghton Mifflin Co. 1891), at 345.

[116] Wilkinson, Charles F. and Anderson, H. Michael, Land and Resource Planning in the National Forests (Island Press 1987), at 134 *quoting* 1908 Annual Report of the Chief Forester at 15.

[117] Every source is different as to Roosevelt's total acreage. Roosevelt himself said he increased the reserves by a factor of two to three. Even by the most conservative figure, however, Roosevelt created more National

Forest acreage than all of the other President's combined.

National Parks and Monuments

[118] Gila Cliff Dwellings – An Administrative History, http://www.nps.gov/gicl/adhi/adhit.htm

[119] Encyclopedia of American Forest and Conservation History, Richard C. Davis Editor (Macmillan Pub. Co. 1983) at 462

[120] Roosevelt, Theodore, Outdoor Pastimes of an American Hunter (1990).

[121] Knue, Joseph, North Dakota Wildlife Viewing Guide (Falcon Press1992).

[122] Burroughs, John, *Camping With President Roosevelt,* The Atlantic Monthly (May 1906).

[123] Miller, Nathan, Theodore Roosevelt, A Life (William Morrow 1992), 39.

[124] Miller, Nathan, Theodore Roosevelt, A Life (William Morrow 1992), 40.

[125] Miller, Nathan, Theodore Roosevelt, A Life (William Morrow 1992), 40.

[126] Roosevelt, Theodore, An Autobiography (1913), Ch. IX

[127] Roosevelt, Theodore, An Autobiography (1913), Ch. XI

[128] Roosevelt, Theodore, Hunting Trips of a Ranchman (1895)

[129] Roosevelt, Theodore, An Autobiography (1913), Ch. IX

[130] Roosevelt, Theodore, An Autobiography (1913), Ch. XI.

[131] Gove, Doris, Audubon Guide to the National Wildlife Refuges-Southeast (Balliett & Fitzgerald 2000).

[132] MacArthur, Loren & Miller, Debbie S., Audubon Guide to the National Wildlife Refuges – Alaska and the Northwest (Balliett &Fitzgerald 2000).